To Remove Your Stress Card

Pierce the protective film with the tip of a pair of scissors. *Carefully* cut a slit across the top, creating an opening through which you can remove the card.

THE DOCTORS' GUIDE TO

INSTANT STRESS RELIEF

THE DOCTORS' GUIDE TO

INSTANT STRESS RELIEF

A PSYCHOLOGICAL AND MEDICAL SYSTEM

Ronald G. Nathan, Ph.D.
Albany Medical College, New York

Thomas E. Staats, Ph.D.
Louisiana State University School of Medicine in Shreveport

Paul J. Rosch, M.D.
The American Institute of Stress, New York

G. P. PUTNAM'S SONS   New York

G. P. Putnam's Sons
Publishers Since 1838
200 Madison Avenue
New York, NY 10016

Design by Carla Weise/Levavi & Levavi
Typeset by Fisher Composition, Inc.

Library of Congress Cataloging-in-Publication Data

Nathan, Ronald G.
The doctors' guide to instant stress relief.

1. Stress (Psychology)—Prevention.   I. Staats,
Thomas E.   II. Rosch, Paul J.   III. Title.
[DNLM: 1. Stress, Psychological—prevention & control—popular
works.   WM 172 N274d]
BF575.S75N37   1987   155.9   87-10754
ISBN 0-399-13296-1

Printed in the United States of America
1   2   3   4   5   6   7   8   9   10

Special recognition is given to the following scientists and writers who have made major contributions to the field of behavioral medicine:

Robert Alberti, Aaron Antonovsky, Herbert Benson, Kenneth Blanchard, Shlomo Breznitz, Barbara Brown, Tom Budzynski, Roy Cameron, Walter Cannon, Edward Charlesworth, Kenneth Cooper, Norman Cousins, Martha Davis, Leonard Derogatis, Robert Eliot, Albert Ellis, Elizabeth Eschelman, George Everly, Jr., Meyer Friedman, Daniel Girdano, Leo Goldberger, Peter Hanson, Nelson Hendler, Thomas Holmes, Edmund Jacobson, Spencer Johnson, Suzanne Kobasa, Daniel Kohli, Arnold Lazarus, Richard Lazarus, Wolfgang Luthe, James Lynch, Salvatore Maddi, James Manuso, John Mason, Joseph Matarazzo, Matthew McKay, Alan McLean, Donald Meichenbaum, Lyle Miller, Neal Miller, Rudolph Moos, David Munz, Kenneth Pelletier, Richard Rahe, Paul Rosenfeld, Ray Rosenman, Johannes Schultz, Gary Schwartz, Mark S. Schwartz, Hans Selye, Charles Spielberger, Johann Stoyva, Charles Stroebel, Alvin Toffler, Dennis Turk, George Whatmore.

> "Therefore say of me that in this book I have only made up a bunch of other people's flowers, and that of my own I have only provided the string that ties them together."
>
> —*Montaigne*

ACKNOWLEDGMENTS

Writing has all the exhilaration and frustration of stress. Many people helped us manage this stress by giving generously and enthusiastically of their time and talent.

Our agent, John Ware, helped us to understand the difficulties of finding a publisher for a book proposal involving a pocket biofeedback device. Nevertheless, he believed in our ideas and took the risks with us. John's hard work and careful guidance led us to Neil Nyren, an innovative and industrious editor with a wonderful sense of humor. Thank you both for all your help and faith in us.

The superb secretarial and administrative support of Ruby Harris and Jeanne Skarina freed us up to write and is deeply appreciated.

We are indebted to Sanford J. Catz, M.Eng., of RCA for the improvements he recommended after using an earlier edition of the *pocket guide*. The photography of Terry Atwood of Shreveport, Louisiana, enhanced both the guide and these pages. Marvin White and his staff at Mid-South Press in Shreveport were most patient with our changes in the *pocket guide*, to the extent of fourteen sets of revisions for the second edition. Their layout and typeface suggestions are also gratefully acknowledged.

Medicomp, Inc., the publishers of Dr. Staats's Stress Vector Analysis gave invaluable support to the standardization and validation of the items in the Seven Minute Stress Test.

Many colleagues and friends read and commented on various

drafts of the manuscript and the *pocket guide*. Special thanks are due to Patricia Cappo, M.S.W., B.C.S.W.; Sue Crow, R.N., M.S.N.; Sanford J. Catz, M.Eng.; Lanny Keller; Terry Kevil, R.N., M.N.Sc.; Kim A. McKinney, R.D.; Dennis Knave, M.D.; Karen Logan; Larry Marr, Ph.D.; Daniel Malmed; Bertha Malmed; Hinda K. Nathan; Kurt C. Nathan, Ph.D.; Myra M. Nathan, Ph.D.; Brent Nick, M.D.; M'Lou Staats, R.N., M.S.N.; and Mary Lynn Vassar, M.S., R.D.

Our patients and workshop participants have been among our best teachers. They taught us what worked and what didn't work for them. Without their feedback, this book would be far more theoretical than useful.

Finally, we want to thank our wives, Myra Nathan, M'Lou Staats, and Marguerite Rosch; and our children, Jennifer and William Nathan, Lauren and Kara Staats, and Donna and Jane Rosch for their love, support, and encouragement.

To our children, who bring us joyful relief

CONTENTS

11

PREFACE

The techniques in this book represent fifty-five years of cumulative experience in the fields of stress and behavioral medicine. As researchers and teachers; directors of biofeedback clinics; and co-authors of textbooks, test manuals, and self-help books, we have often been frustrated by a major deficiency in existing stress books. Either they describe only one technique—which may or may not work for the reader's particular stress problems—or they present an overwhelming maze of techniques, difficult to choose from and difficult to follow. Many readers find these books simply too confusing to use.

This book is different, and we hope it meets your needs. It contains the best of the brief, clinically proven techniques for dividing and relieving stress that we have developed in our work. Even more to the point, these are *rapid, simple* strategies that anyone can follow.

We have found these strategies very effective, not only in our offices but also in the corporate seminars we have conducted for AT&T, Blue Cross/Blue Shield, Merrill Lynch, and other clients. Our patients improve when they use them. Our workshop participants report that these are the techniques they use most frequently to relieve their stress successfully.

Are they truly "instant"? We believe they are. Most of the prescriptions are designed to be used immediately, at the very moment of stress, so people can avoid stress's cumulative effects and even benefit from its positive power. From the "six-second tranquilizer" to "red-light relaxation," the results can be felt at once and continue to be felt.

In addition, the feedback supplied moment-to-moment by the unique *pocket guide* found in this book provides a continuous, accurate monitoring of your stress and immediate information on how it is being alleviated as you use the techniques we describe.

A NOTE ON THE INSTANT POCKET GUIDE

We are very conscious of the value of biofeedback devices as tools for relaxation training, but we have always been so disappointed by the credit-card type of stress and biofeedback devices available on the market that we have never been able to recommend them in our practice.

Typically, the user presses his thumb on a temperature-sensitive sensor cell and then, after several seconds, lifts his thumb to read off the stress level indicated by the cell. The accuracy of this method is highly limited, however; and since the crystals begin giving incorrect readings within a second or two after the thumb is removed, the design of these cards makes it impossible to detect positive or negative temperature change over time—and thus to gauge the user's progress.

As one of our patients complained, it's like shooting at a target and being unable to see where the arrows are landing.

To remedy this situation, we devised a new card. By improving the sensitivity of the sensors, calibrating them to within a half-degree accuracy, and constructing the cards so that the finger can be pressed *underneath* the sensors, we have made it possible to read off temperature and stress levels even as they register.

You now get continuous biofeedback with double the range and twice the accuracy. We have also added the extra flaps on the card to give you a quick guide to a dozen brief prescriptions for stress relief.

THE SEVEN-MINUTE STRESS TEST

Another feature of this book is the Seven-Minute Stress Test. It was developed by one of the authors, Thomas Staats, Ph.D., from two much more comprehensive tests also devised by him for professional use—the Stress Vector Analysis Test Battery and the Corporate and Personal Stress Inventory—and appears here in print for the first time.

This test is designed to break down the sources of your stress into one or more of three key areas: your body, your mind, and your situation. Suffering from headaches, ulcers, back pain? The stress may be in your body. Do you feel nervous, blue, have difficulty sleeping or concentrating? The stress may be in your mind. Are you under heavy pressure at work or at home, feel unstimulated in your job, unsatisfied with your social life, or in upheaval over a change of habit—smoking, drinking, or eating, for instance? The stress may be in your situation. The remedies for each source may be dramatically different.

The Seven-Minute Stress Test will help you diagnose just where your problems lie and, consequently, which of the self-improvement strategies mapped out in the following chapters are most appropriate for your needs. By mixing and matching—selecting the set of solutions that best fits your individual needs—you will be able to achieve maximum results.

This test has more scientifically validated predictive power than any stress test currently available in any other self-help book. We are sure it will be valuable for many people.

For further help, an appendix recommends self-help books and recordings for each source of stress. These can be used to expand and deepen what you gain from this book.

AN IMPORTANT WARNING

If you suffer from a stress-related mental or physical disorder, consult your doctor or mental health professional. The brief techniques presented here are excellent adjuncts to stress-management training and valuable tools for maintenance, but they are not substitutes for professional care.

To that end, we also provide chapters devoted to helping you find and form a partnership for health with your physician, as well as to find professionals certified to provide biofeedback.

Many colleagues, patients, and workshop participants have read drafts of this book or used earlier editions of the *pocket guide*. They report benefits well beyond stress relief, and their enthusiasm inspired us to write this book. We hope you will join them and find even more than the instant relief you seek.

Ronald G. Nathan
Thomas E. Staats
Paul J. Rosch

A Quick Guide to
The Pocket Stress Card

USING YOUR POCKET GUIDE*'S QUICK TEST FOR TEMPERATURE*

On your *pocket guide* there is a black plastic square that is made up of four sensor cells. If you carry the guide in a warm pocket and the square is not all black, allow the cells a few seconds to cool and return to black.

Place your right thumb over the black plastic square as shown in figure 1. Press lightly and count slowly to ten. It takes about ten seconds to activate the guide's heat sensors.

Remove your thumb and quickly find the *lowest-numbered sensor cell showing a color other than black*. Ignore the higher numbered cells, even if they show a color. Read the description of your stress level next to the lowest numbered cell you found with a color other than black. For example, in figure 2, the lowest-numbered cell showing a color other than black reads 2. The corresponding description reads "partly relaxed."

Figure 1: Thumb positioned

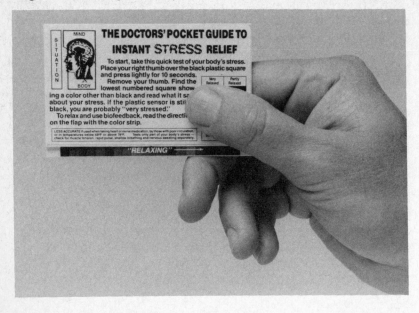

IF YOU TAKE THE QUICK TEST AND THE SQUARE REMAINS ALL BLACK

Most stress and biofeedback cards only register a 10- or 11-degree range of temperature and start at about 85 degrees F. When people are stressed and use such cards, their hands are usually cooler than 85 degrees and they get no feedback. Your *pocket guide* was designed to overcome this problem. It has a 20-degree range and starts at 75 degrees F. However, if after ten seconds, the square remains all black, and you are viewing it in a well-lit area, your finger temperature is below 75 degrees. You are probably very stressed.

The quick test is only a limited test of stress. As your guide warns, it is "less accurate if used when taking heart or nerve medication, by those with poor circulation, or in temperatures below 68 degrees F or above 74 degrees F. It tests only part of your body's stress—check for muscle tension, rapid pulse, shallow breathing, and nervous sweating separately."

Even if your quick test is not completely accurate, you can still benefit from learning how to use relative changes in the heat sensor for biofeedback.

Figure 2: The lowest-numbered sensor showing a color other than black reads 2 in this illustration. The corresponding description reads "partly relaxed."

THE DOCTORS' POCKET GUIDE TO
INSTANT STRESS RELIEF

To start, take this quick test of your body's stress. Place your right thumb over the black plastic square and press lightly for 10 seconds. Remove your thumb. Find the lowest numbered square showing a color other than black and read what it says about your stress. If the plastic sensor is still all black, you are probably "very stressed."

To relax and use biofeedback, read the directions on the flap with the color strip.

LESS ACCURATE if used when taking heart or nerve medication, by those with poor circulation, or in temperatures below 68ºF or above 74ºF.   Tests only part of your body's stress — check for muscle tension, rapid pulse, shallow breathing and nervous sweating separately.

You have probably used biofeedback at one time or another. Does this surprise you? Have you ever been on a diet and stood on a bathroom scale to see if you had lost or gained weight? If so, you have used a form of biofeedback.

WHAT IS BIOFEEDBACK?

If you break the word into its three parts—*bio–feed–back*—you can see that it has to do with machines that give (*feed*) useful information about living (*bio*logical) tissues by returning (*back*) the information to its source. In the case of your weight, the scale gives you back information about your living tissue—how *much* living tissue you have.

When you stand on a bathroom scale and the meter stops on a number, it gives you "feedback" about your weight. If you are dissatisfied with the reading on the dial, you know it may be time for some changes in your diet and exercise program.

BIOFEEDBACK AND THE STRESS RESPONSE

Biofeedback can help us change some biological events that are undesirable for our bodies. For example, the heat-sensitive biofeedback cells on your *pocket guide* can help you learn to relax when stress would be unhealthy.

As you may know, cold hands are usually a sign of stress and warm hands a sign of relaxation. Temperature-sensitive devices can measure the changes and give you feedback about them for your use.

Part of the stress response takes blood away from the stomach, hands, and feet. It is then redistributed to the large muscle groups to provide the fuel needed for running and pushing. As you may know or will learn in chapter 1, the stress response is often called the fight-or-flight response. Under stress, the thigh and shoulder muscles get three to four times as much blood as they do at rest. As blood leaves your hands, they get colder.

That is why cold hands are usually a sign of anxiety and warm hands a sign of relaxation. These changes are an important and useful part of your body's nervous system. Temperature-sensitive devices can measure the changes and give you feedback about them for your use.

YOUR BIOFEEDBACK GUIDE

Effective biofeedback training requires rapid, accurate, and ongoing feedback of changes in your body. You can use the *pocket guide* or other popular stress cards as tests of your body's stress by placing your thumb over the cell(s) and then removing your thumb to read the temperature. However, such stress tests are a very limited form of biofeedback.

Most cards have limited value because the crystals begin giving incorrect readings within a second or two after the thumb is removed. In addition, if you try leaving your thumb in place to improve accuracy, you cannot see positive or negative temperature changes.

Fortunately, your *pocket guide* and other biofeedback devices can give you immediate, accurate, and continuous feedback to help you gain greater mastery over your autonomic nervous system.

GETTING YOUR FINGERS INTO POSITION FOR BIOFEEDBACK

Your *pocket guide* has been specially designed so you can place the pad of your right index finger *under* the black plastic piece containing the four sensor squares. This placement allows you to read immediate and accurate feedback over time.

To use your guide for biofeedback, you will fold the guide as shown in figure 3. As you can see, the folds you will make are also illustrated for quick reference in the lower left corner on the inside of your *pocket guide*.

Figure 3: Folding your *pocket guide* for biofeedback

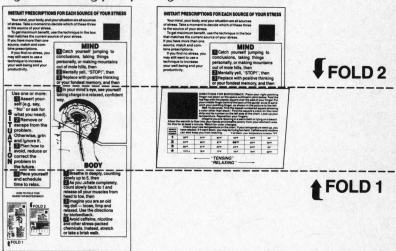

Start by making fold 1. Then place your right index finger nail down on the space outlined in pink on the panel with the color strip, as shown in figure 4.

Now, fold the top panel that encases the black sensor cells over the pad of your right index finger. Then put your middle finger behind the back of the guide—that is, sandwich your pointing finger between the color strip panel and the panel with the sensor squares.

Ensure total contact with the squares by lightly pressing the lower corner of what has now become the front panel with your thumb, as shown in figure 5 and on the color strip panel of the guide. This is the best position for biofeedback.

Figure 4: Finger in position for fold 2 and the sensor

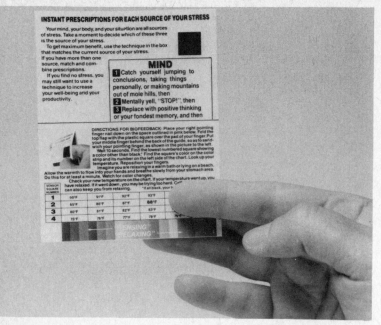

Be sure to leave a clear view of the top of the four squares. Then wait ten seconds and find the lowest numbered square that is not black.

READING YOUR TEMPERATURE BEFORE BIOFEEDBACK

To look up your beginning temperature for a biofeedback session, please refer to the chart on the panel with the color strip of your *pocket guide*. Find the lowest-numbered square that is not black on the chart under the words *Sensor Square Number*.

If you were unable to keep your finger positioned under the sensor squares while you were looking up the cell number this time, reposition your finger and press the guide firmly down on it for another ten seconds.

Now, look at the color of the lowest-numbered square and find it on the color strip. Next, go across from the square number and up from this color on the strip to find your beginning temperature for this biofeedback session.

The colors registering on your sensor may be slightly different

Figure 5: Fingers positioned for biofeedback

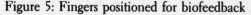

from the shades shown on your *guide*'s color strip. These differences result from variations in dye lots of liquid crystals and should not affect the relative accuracy of your readings.

If you want to compare your finger temperature to the "normal" or average temperature, we have put 88 degrees F in bold numbers on the chart. For many reasons, finger temperature is not as stable as other temperatures commonly used in medicine. However, the largest study we found gave 88 degrees as an average finger temperature.

CHARTING YOUR PROGRESS

To help you keep records of your progress, there is a biofeedback training chart at the end of this book. You may want to take a moment now to put your beginning temperature in the "before" square on the chart.

Please note that the *pocket guide* is not completely accurate if used in places that are considerably warmer or colder than normal room temperature. Practicing in different places may affect the temperatures you chart, but the changes in temperature during any one session would still be fairly accurate.

Fortunately, when you use biofeedback, these changes are more important than the actual temperature of your fingers. Similarly, if your initial temperature is higher because of medication or lower because of circulatory problems, increases in temperature still add up to stress relief.

To raise your temperature and complete this introductory biofeedback session, follow the Directions for Biofeedback on your card but start with the blue paragraph next to the photograph. When you complete the session, put your new temperature in the "After" square on the chart at the end of this book.

This has been only a quick guide to using the pocket stress card, so that you can become familiar with it right away. For more detailed information on its use for biofeedback, especially if your temperature went down instead of up, please consult chapter 13, Using Biofeedback.

Stress is the spice of life. . . . Who would enjoy a life of no runs, no hits, no errors?

—Hans Selye, M.D.
Stress without Distress

Teach me the art of taking minute vacations—of slowing down to look at a flower, to chat with a friend, to pat a dog, to answer a child's question, to read a few lines from a good book. . . . The race is not always to the swift—there is more to life than increasing its speed.

—Kenneth Grooms

Stress:
Symptoms,
Sources,
and
Solutions

1

Stress Starts in Seconds

What Is Stress?

Have you ever felt that the faster you go, the behinder you get? Have you ever found yourself in a family quarrel that made you feel sad, mad, or bad all over? Have you ever been irritable because of a headache, backache, or stomachache?

If you answered yes to any of these questions, then you have experienced stress. We all have. The only people who no longer have stress in their lives are in their graves. If stress is a part of life, what's the problem?

Stress can make you miserable. It can make you so scared that everything seems frightening. It can make you so angry that you can't even think straight. It can even make you sick enough to land in the hospital.

What is stress? Many people use the word to describe anything bad or unpleasant, and even professionals disagree. There are over a dozen different definitions of stress in the scientific journals.

An Instant Definition of Stress

Imagine that you are a cave dweller. You are sitting in front of your cave fire, enjoying its warmth, when up comes the shadow of a saber-toothed tiger!

In a few seconds, your breathing quickens, your heart races, and your blood pressure soars. Blood drains rapidly from your hands and feet into your thigh and shoulder muscles. Butterflies seem to invade your stomach, perspiration floods your skin, and your muscles tense up for fight or flight. This reaction is called the stress response.

This response brings oxygen and nutrients to the large muscles and the brain for a surge of energy and alertness. Digestion slows, so you get the butterflies. Perspiration cools your overheating body. When blood leaves your hands, they get cold as well as clammy. Tense muscles prepare you for rapid action.

The stress response was very adaptive for cave dwellers, but today we have few physical battles to fight and almost nowhere to run. Instead, we have angry bosses, impossible deadlines, final exams, snarled traffic, burned toast, and screaming children.

From Seconds to Years of Stress

The stress response starts in seconds. Too many stressful minutes can lead to an exhausting day. If you have the response intensely and repeatedly over weeks and months, stress begins to attack your health and happiness. The toll over the years can be enormous.

Instant stress relief is important because it can keep your stress from accumulating and overwhelming you. It also allows you to tap into the power of stress as an exhilarating force in your life.

But first, let's look at the dark side of stress—when it builds up and becomes a destructive force.

2

Stress Symptoms and Disease

The American Academy of Family Physicians estimates that 60 percent of the problems brought to physicians in this country are stress-related. Many are the result of stress; others are made worse or last longer because of it.

Every week, 95 million Americans suffer some stress-related symptom and take some medication for these aches and pains.

Stress and its symptoms also interfere with productivity. Each year, American business loses an estimated $150 billion to stress-related problems.

Furthermore, stress can disrupt close relationships, and research suggests that loneliness can be lethal.

The ways we cope with stress and loneliness can lead to a lifestyle of harmful habits such as overeating, overdrinking, and smoking. Eating, drinking, and even smoking can all temporarily lower our arousal and anxiety levels. Each can make us feel pleasantly drowsy, but they have their long-term costs.

Is Your Life-style Killing You?

A study at the University of Tennessee Medical School determined that more than half its hospital's admissions could have been prevented by changes in life-styles. If we want to reduce the economic and human costs of illness, we need to do something about our overeating, overdrinking, smoking, underexercising, and time-urgent living.

What do these life-style changes have to do with instant stress relief? Everyone makes life-style decisions moment-to-moment. To eat or not to eat; to rush or not to rush; and so on, through every hour of our lives.

You can choose a life-style rather than a death-style. The best choices can become almost automatic, but you still make the choices and relieve the stress one moment at a time.

A Checklist of Stress Symptoms

The following list will help you decide if you are making healthy choices—or if you are among the 95 million Americans who suffer from one or more stress-related symptoms each week.

Some of these symptoms may surprise you. Many people accept these conditions as part of modern life. Others become so accustomed to the symptoms that they tune them out almost completely.

We believe little things can make or break your relief of stress. By responding upstream to your body's smaller stress signals, we hope you can avoid the bigger ones downstream.

Many stress symptoms affect most people every once in a while, or to a small extent. If you experience some of these symptoms part of the time and to a mild degree, you are probably just responding the way most people do to our stressful world. Instant stress relief may be just what you need to enhance your health.

On the other hand, if you experience a good number of these symptoms in a severe way and a great deal of the time, it is important to see your doctor. The disorder is likely to be stress-related—but some physical diseases only wear the mask of stress. Only your physician should be trusted to make a medical diagnosis.

The stress symptoms are listed under four main categories. The categories make sense medically and psychologically, but the headings are a little technical. If they are confusing to you, just treat them as good places to take a break as you go through the list.

STRESS SYMPTOMS

Physical Symptoms of Distress Involving Skeletal Muscles

1. Tension headaches
2. Frowning
3. Gritting or grinding of teeth
4. Jaw pain
5. Stuttering or stammering
6. Trembling of lips or hands
7. Muscle tenseness, bracing, and aches
8. Neck aches
9. Back pain
10. Aggressive body language

Physical Symptoms of Distress Involving the Autonomic Nervous System

1. Migraine headaches
2. Increased sensitivity to light and sound
3. Lightheadedness, faintness, or dizziness
4. Ringing in ears
5. Enlarged pupils
6. Blushing
7. Dry mouth
8. Problems swallowing
9. Frequent colds or bouts with the flu
10. Hives
11. Rashes
12. "Cold chills" or "goose bumps"
13. Heartburn, stomach cramping, or nausea
14. Uneven or rapid heartbeat without exercising
15. Difficulty breathing
16. Sudden, suffocating panic, as if you are about to die

17. Heart and chest pain
18. Increased perspiration
19. Night sweats
20. Cold, sweaty hands
21. Painfully cold hands and feet
22. Gaseousness or belching
23. Frequent urination
24. Constipation
25. Nervous diarrhea
26. Lowered sexual desire
27. Difficulty with sexual orgasm

Mental Symptoms of Distress

1. Anxiety, worry, guilt, or nervousness
2. Increased anger and frustration
3. Moodiness
4. Depression
5. Increased or decreased appetite
6. Racing thoughts
7. Nightmares
8. Problems concentrating
9. Trouble learning new information
10. Forgetfulness
11. Disorganization or confusion
12. Difficulty making decisions
13. A sense of being overloaded or overwhelmed by problems
14. More frequent crying
15. Suicidal thoughts
16. Fear of getting close to people
17. Loneliness

Behavioral Symptoms of Distress

1. Inattention to dress or grooming
2. More frequent lateness
3. A more "serious" appearance
4. Unusual behaviors
5. Nervous habits, such as finger or foot tapping
6. Rushing around or pacing the floor

7. Increased frustration and irritability
8. Edginess
9. Overreaction to small things
10. Increased number of minor accidents
11. Perfectionism
12. Reduced work efficiency or productivity
13. Lies or excuses to cover up poor work
14. Fast or mumbled speech
15. Defensiveness or suspiciousness
16. Strained communication with others
17. Social withdrawal
18. Constant tiredness
19. Sleep problems
20. Frequent use of over-the-counter drugs
21. Weight gain or loss without diet
22. Increased smoking
23. Recreational drug use
24. Increased alcohol use
25. Gambling or overspending

Now that you know something about stress and its effects on your life, we want to help you divide and conquer it. The next chapter shows you how to separate the sources of your stress into three categories, so you can choose the best instant treatments for overcoming them.

3

The Three Sources of Stress

Where does stress come from? What triggers the stress response? The answer is *anything*—if you perceive it as dangerous or demanding.

The sources of stress can be divided into three basic categories: your *situation*, your *mind*, and your *body*.*

Stress from Your Situation

This category includes all the outside demands of people and things around you. Where you live, the air you breathe, the sounds you hear, and the people you know can all trigger the emergency, fight-or-flight response.

Many people think that all stress comes from the situations in their lives. They may have windowless workplaces, with too many bosses, children who seem to take turns playing wake-up at night, or cars that stay in the shop more often than in their garages.

---

*By dividing stress into situation, mind, and body, we are only supporting a mind–body split insofar as it helps you to choose the most effective treatment(s).

These delights of modern life are abundant sources of stress, but two other sources are equally important.

Stress from Your Body

What we do *to* our bodies and what we do *for* our bodies often determine what our bodies will do for us and what our bodies will do in response to other sources of stress.

Getting too little sleep, eating irregular meals, or working too many hours are all stressful for our bodies. Coffee, tea, colas, nicotine, salt, and sugar are packed with stress-inducing chemicals, and each can trigger the fight-or-flight response. Physical illnesses and pain, including stress-related disorders, are also prime sources.

Stress from Your Mind

And then there is the mind. What we think can trigger stress. Shakespeare said it in *Hamlet:* "Things are neither good nor bad, but thinking makes it so." If we jump to conclusions, take things personally, or exaggerate our problems, we will react as if things are dangerous and trigger the emergency response.

There are many other stressful ways of thinking. The *shoulds, oughts, musts, have tos, owes,* and *deserves* of life can be very stressful. These thoughts can make us oversensitive, guilt-prone, time-urgent, or depressed.

To review the three major sources of stress, take a look at the diagram below. As you can see, your situational stress is outside your body and comes to your attention mainly through your eyes or ears. Your mind's stress comes from what's going on inside your head. Your body's stress comes mainly from your neck down and from what you do to your body.

A Smashing Example of the Three Sources of Stress

Imagine that you are driving along in your brand-new car on a two-lane highway. It is a beautiful spring day, and you are feeling great. Then you hear the screech of tires as the cars in front of you

Figure 6: The three sources of stress

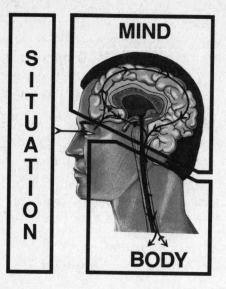

slam on their brakes. Each car comes closer and closer to rear-ending the next one.

Within seconds, the stress of the situation enters your mind through your eyes and ears. Your mind responds electrically and chemically in several ways. The middle and lower portions of your brain electrically trigger a massive fight-or-flight response. All this happens before you can even think about the situation and say to yourself, "Oh, my goodness, not my new car!"

Your foot slams on the brake. You grip the wheel and try to straighten out.

Your body dumps sugars and fats into your bloodstream for quick energy and strength. Other chemicals prepare your blood to clot more quickly, to reduce possible blood loss. You feel your heart pounding in your chest and temples. Your brain is receiving more oxygen to sharpen your senses and your coordination.

More Stress—Some Good, Some Bad

The loud screech of tires around you has not ceased, and you look up into your rear-view mirror. A car is quickly approaching your back bumper.

These perceptions and thoughts in the upper part of your brain also send stimulation to the lower brain. As you can see, the body's stress response is triggered by several pathways in your brain.

The brain electrically triggers the fight-or-flight response, but it also activates chemical messages. These messages stimulate the release of a powerful substance that can put the body on alert for longer periods of time. A steady drip of this alerting chemical can corrode and exhaust the body.

Let's say you survived with only minor injuries, but your new car was totaled. The accident was an event outside yourself. It came from your situation. Later, if you keep thinking about what happened, the accident becomes a powerful mind stressor. That is, unless you have replacement insurance and enjoy disruptions in your routine.

The Two-Way Street of Stress

Let's say you mentally upset yourself and can't fall asleep. You might suffer stress-related disorders of the body, such as sleeplessness or muscle tension. If you then become concerned about these disorders, you will experience still more stress from your mind.

Notice that in figure 6 the arrows in the neck point both down and up. These arrows represent this two-way street of stress.

Choosing the Best Coping Tools

Knowing where stress comes from will help you choose the best tools for relieving it. If you cannot go to sleep because of tense muscles, the source of your stress is your body. A relaxation technique from the section in this book about relieving the body's stress could be your best bet.

If you are worrying about something that happened yesterday or might happen tomorrow, your stress is coming from your mind. Realizing this, you might relieve it by using the section introducing rapid thought-stopping and thought-improvement.

If the problem is an angry customer who has given you an impossible deadline, the stress is coming from your outside situation. The most effective strategies will probably be the instant communication skills or time-management tools in the section about change strategies for your situational stress.

Finally, in the last section of the book, you will learn powerful ways of combining strategies to optimize your overall results.

4

And Now, a Few Words from Our Sponsor: The Good News About Stress

Knowledge is power. Now that you know what stress is and where it comes from, we have some very good news for you. Not all stress is harmful: Stress without distress is very real.

The fight-or-flight response can be distressful, but it can also give us our zest and excitement for living, our enthusiasm and energy for getting things done. We even pay for stress: Adventure movies, bumper cars, strenuous sports—the list goes on. Few of us would want to give up all of life's thrills to go meditate on some mountain-top and watch life go by.

Peak Performance and the Stress Curve

Just as you can suffer from burnout, you can suffer from rustout. Not only can a boring job actually increase your odds of heart disease, but at very low levels of stress, people are rarely involved or productive. As pressure and stress rise, productivity increases up to the point of peak performance. If more stress is added, the individual becomes overloaded and productivity starts dropping off.

You can see how productivity shifts in figure 7. The optimal range of productive stress is in the middle of too little and too much. You want to be alert and alive, but not overwhelmed.

Figure 7: The relationship between productivity and stress

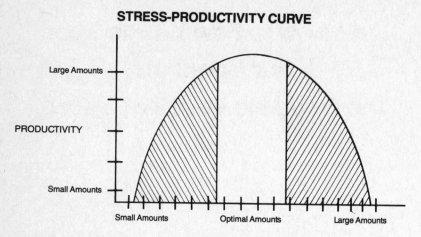

STRESS-PRODUCTIVITY CURVE

TIME, ENERGY AND STRESS

Using Stress for Productivity and Pleasure

This relationship between stress and productivity is the reason that we do not want to relieve all or even most of our stress. We can optimize productivity and pleasure by learning how much stress is too much and by relieving that which is unnecessary and irritating.

A mining executive summed it up this way: "Stress is like an explosive—you have to use it or defuse it."

A powerful first step in relieving your excess stress is to measure it. The next section will help you do just that.

II

Measuring Your Stress with a Seven-Minute Test

5

Measuring Your Stress

Judging the impact of stress in your life may be difficult. Many people learn to live with unhealthy levels of tension because it builds up very gradually, minute by minute, over years.

Is Stress Creeping Up On You?

Stress is like ivy growing up a tree. At first, the tree hardly responds. The ivy creeps up its trunk and digs into the weak spots in its bark. Then the ivy starts to cover over the branches and crowd the leaves of the tree. Eventually, the ivy strangles the tree by cutting it off from life-giving light and moisture. Stress can creep up on us in very much the same way.

Almost everyone is aware of certain periods of extreme stress or distress, but most people underestimate its cumulative effects. Many of our patients who are referred by their physicians for stress-related disorders tell us that they are not aware of being under any more stress than anyone else.

Such cases remind us of the little girl on her first day of school

54

who was looking at a book, her nose about three inches from the pages. Her teacher asked if she was having trouble seeing. The girl calmly replied, "There's nothing wrong with my eyes." From her point of view, she could see as well as anyone else. She assumed that the rest of the world saw things with blurry edges, too.

The Long and Short of Stress Testing

You may know you are under stress, but do you know how much? A number of excellent stress tests are available to mental health professionals, but they are time-consuming, expensive, and require advanced training to interpret.

There are also many tests available in popular books about stress, but unfortunately most of the ones we found have no scientific validity. Some books include a thoroughly researched life-event questionnaire, but even that predicts less than 10 percent of typical health problems.

To give you a ballpark estimate of your stress, we have created a short test using items from a newer professional instrument. The longer test is used at such institutions as Baylor and the Mayo Clinic, as well as in stress clinics and in industrial settings here and abroad.

The results from this short form are close enough to those of the longer test to be of considerable use to you. To read about the predictive power of the short Seven-Minute Stress Test, turn to appendix I. As far as we know, it has more scientifically validated predictive power of past and current health problems than any stress test currently available in any other self-help book.

The longer test is called the Stress Vector Analysis Test Battery (SVA). You may have already taken it in a clinic or at work. If so, you have a choice. You may skip to chapter 8, "Using Your Stress Scores to Weigh Your Alternatives," or you may update your scores by taking the short form which follows.

Measuring Your Three Sources of Stress

There is an additional benefit of taking either this short test or the longer Stress Vector Analysis test. Not only will both measure your overall stress level, but they will also help you assess the amount of stress coming from each of those three main sources: mind, body, and situation.

Avoiding the Stress of Changing Too Much Too Quickly

Change in any area of your life can be stressful. In fact, one of the earliest and best-known stress tests focused on major life changes. These changes included both desirable and undesirable changes—both marriage and divorce, for example. Studies showed that the higher your life-changes score, the more likely you were to become ill in the future.

Later research challenged these findings. People with certain traits, to be described later in this book, were found to be quite resistant to the ill effects of major life change. Other studies suggested that the day-to-day hassles created by such changes as marriage might explain why even desirable change can be stressful. In addition, daily hassles appear to be more predictive of illness than do major life changes.

Such research supports the importance of relieving your stress throughout the day with quick techniques—but, since change can easily create hassles, it is also important not to make too many changes at one time. The test you are about to take assesses many of life's hassles and is designed to help you decide *where* to make changes, so you can avoid the stress of changing too much too quickly.

There are three parts to the test, each part measuring one of the three sources of stress.

The Three Scales of the Test

The three scales ask different types of questions in different ways, so please be sure to read carefully the instructions to each. Take your time, be honest with yourself, and, if in doubt, go with what seems to describe your experience the best.

This test was originally developed for people who work outside the home. If you are a full-time homemaker, you may wish to answer the questions about work by describing the work you do at home. Spouses and parents are not supervisors, but complaints about your homemaking from your spouse or your parents can be substituted for those of supervisors where applicable.

This test may not be as accurate for homemakers as for those who work outside the home. Every test's accuracy is limited when it is used by people for whom norms are not available. Even if you are a homemaker, however, the test should give you a rough estimate of your stress.

6

The Seven-Minute Stress Test*

The Stress in Your Situation Scale

Directions: On a separate piece of paper, number from 1 to 42. Read each stress problem below. If the problem causes you no difficulty, pressure, concern, or stress, put a *1* next to the problem's number. If the problem causes you light, moderate, heavy, or extreme stress, put the corresponding number from the chart below next to the problem's number.

1. *No* stress, pressure, difficulty, or concern.
2. *Light* stress, pressure, difficulty, or concern
3. *Moderate* stress, pressure, difficulty, or concern
4. *Heavy* stress, pressure, difficulty, or concern
5. *Extreme, almost intolerable* stress, pressure, difficulty, or concern

* ©1985, 1986 Doctor's Psychological Center, Inc.

1. Feeling pressures at work from one or more superiors
2. Sensing a heavy pressure to produce
3. Sensing a heavy pressure to produce beyond reasonable limits
4. Having personality clashes with superiors
5. Feeling pressures from having more work than I can reasonably handle (extremely heavy product/service demand)
6. Feeling pressures from not having enough work (extremely poor product/service demand)
7. Having criticism directed at me/my department from inside the organization
8. Feeling unstimulated by my job
9. Being held responsible without having real control in my organization
10. Feeling inadequate in my present position
11. Feeling uneasy about an impending promotion or job change
12. Feeling that my innovative ideas are ignored
13. Feeling underpaid, undercompensated, or unappreciated
14. Feeling that other co-workers are treated better within the organization than I am and for no apparent reason
15. Feeling inferior or self-conscious in comparison to my co-workers
16. Encountering noise pollution or excess distractions on the job
17. Feeling stress from heavy labor on the job, or dangerous or poor working conditions
18. Feeling loneliness or lack of affection and support in my life
19. Feeling unsatisfied over my present marital situation
20. Feeling unsatisfied over my present sex life
21. Feeling frustrated because of my children's behavior
22. Having financial pressures
23. Having legal difficulties
24. Having arguments or discord with spouse/lover
25. Worrying about compatibility within the family
26. Worrying about my relationship with my spouse's/lover's parents
27. Worrying about the amount and quality of my social life
28. Feeling a general lack of shared family activities

29. Getting criticism from my spouse/lover
30. Getting criticism from my extended family, including ex-spouses and in-laws, if applicable
31. Getting criticism from friends
32. Feeling frustrated about having too little time to complete home projects
33. Having difficulty getting enough personal recreation/fun
34. Feeling pressured by thoughts about an affair on my part or that of my spouse/lover
35. Worrying about religion
36. Worrying about drug/alcohol problems within my family
37. Worrying about the chronic health or mental health problems of myself or my family
38. Feeling bored or trapped in my home situation
39. Feeling that I don't get enough time to myself
40. Being in the midst of habit change (for example, dieting, stopping smoking or drinking)
41. Feeling dissatisfied with my appearance
42. Feeling dissatisfied with my spouse's/lover's appearance or habits

When you have completed the test, add up your responses to questions 1 to 42 above for your subtotal for situational stress.

The Stress in Your Body Scale

Directions: Number from 43 to 53 on your answer sheet. Read each disorder listed below. Answer yes if, according to your doctor, you *currently* have trouble with the disorder. Answer no if you do not. Find the number next to your yes or no answer and put it next to the disorder's number.

43. Ulcer (burning stomach pain)
    Yes = 10; No = 1
44. Spastic colon (lower gut cramping/pain)
    Yes = 10; No = 1
45. Colitis (lower gut pain and infection)
    Yes = 5; No = 1

46. Gastric hyperacidity (heartburn)
    Yes = 10; No = 1
47. Diarrhea when upset
    Yes = 10; No = 1
48. Muscle aches
    Yes = 5; No = 1
49. Mental disorder
    Yes = 10; No = 1
50. Headaches, tension
    Yes = 10; No = 1
51. Headaches, migraine
    Yes = 5; No = 1
52. Back pain
    Yes = 10; No = 1
53. Hives or rashes
    Yes = 5; No = 1

When you have completed the test, add up your responses to questions 43 to 53 above for your subtotal for stress from your body.

The Stress in Your Mind Scale

Directions: Number from 54 to 63 on your answer sheet. Read each of the common stress problems below. If the problem has caused you no difficulty or distress in the past two weeks, put a *1* next to its number. If the problem has caused you a little, a mild amount, a moderate amount, or a severe amount of distress, put the corresponding number from the chart below next to the problem's number.

1. *No* distress
2. A *little* distress
3. *Mild* distress
4. *Moderate* distress
5. *Severe* distress

54. Having troubling thoughts that keep coming to mind
55. Having difficulty concentrating

56. Never being satisfied with your performance
57. Feeling nervous, uptight, keyed-up, or "hyper"
58. Having spells of shakiness, weakness, faintness, or pounding heart
59. Feeling low, discouraged, or blue
60. Feeling so drained that everything is an effort
61. Having problems with sleeping
62. Worrying about things now or about the future
63. Feeling angry and impatient

When you have completed the test, add up your responses to questions 54 to 63 above for your subtotal for stress from your mind.

7

Scoring the
Seven-Minute Stress Test

S coring the Seven-Minute Stress Test is not difficult, especially if you have a hand calculator. If you do not have one, take your time and add up the numbers carefully.

Go back to the first part of the test called the Stress in Your Situation Scale. Add up all the points for questions 1 through 42.

Next, go on to the part called the Stress in Your Body Scale and add up the points for questions 43 through 53.

Now it is time to add up your score for the Stress in Your Mind Scale. Add up the points for questions 54 through 63.

List these subtotals separately.

Converting the Subtotals to Percentile Scores

To use the subtotals, we need to convert them to percentile ranks. A percentile rank is a number that compares your stress to that of any 100 other people taking the test. Unlike an achievement test, a low score on this stress test is generally better than a high score.

To convert your subtotal scores to percentile ranks, refer to the tables in appendix I and write the values on your answer sheet.

Now add up the three percentile ranks you found in the tables. Look up the total of the ranks that you just calculated in the last table in appendix I and put the value on your answer sheet.

Translating Percentile Scores into Easier-to-Understand Sentences

Please write the four statements below on your answer sheet and fill in the blanks using your percentile ranks above.

Example: My percentile score on the Stress in Your Situation Scale was 86. Therefore, my situational stress level is higher than those of 86 out of every 100 people who have taken this scale.

My percentile score on the Stress in Your Situation Scale was ___. Therefore, I am experiencing more stress from my situation at this time than ___ out of every 100 people who have taken this scale.

My percentile score on the Stress in Your Body Scale was ___. Therefore, I am experiencing more stress from my body at this time than ___ out of every 100 people who have taken this scale.

My percentile score on the Stress in Your Mind Scale was ___. Therefore, I am experiencing more stress from my mind at this time than ___ out of every 100 people who have taken this scale.

My total stress level percentile score was ___. Therefore, I am experiencing more total stress at this time than ___ out of every 100 persons who have taken this test.

You now know how much stress you are experiencing compared to how much stress others face. In addition, you now know where most of your stress comes from. The higher the score in each area, the more you may want to practice the stress-relief strategies that work best to reduce that particular source.

The next chapter will explain in greater detail the meaning of your percentile scores. It will also help you decide the best way to relieve your stress.

8

Using Your Stress Scores to Weigh Your Alternatives

The following chart will help you understand the meaning of your percentile ranks in a little different way.

PERCENTILE RANK	MEANING
1–45	Desirable level of stress
46–66	Average level of stress
67–84	High average (mild) level of stress
85–93	Moderate level of stress
Above 93	High level of stress

Desirable or Average Levels of Stress

If you scored below the sixty-sixth percentile on all the scales, you probably do not have a serious problem with stress. You may want to find your highest scale and use the matching stress-relief strategies to enhance your pleasure or productivity in that area of your life. On the other hand, your low scores may indicate boredom and you may find it best to seek more stimulating experiences.

Your systematic use of techniques for instant stress relief will probably go beyond treating or even preventing stress-related symptoms and into the exciting new frontier of health promotion and wellness.

A workshop participant with a great deal of stress asked the low-scoring person next to him why he was wasting his time with the course. The response? "You don't have to be sick to get better!"

Mild to Moderate Levels of Stress

If you scored above the eighty-fourth percentile on any of the three scales of this test or those of the SVA, then you have a stress problem of sufficient importance to warrant serious study and mastery of the system described in this book. You could benefit from using the system many times throughout the day.

If you scored above the sixty-sixth percentile on any one scale, stress problems from that source are the ones you probably encounter most often. Research and clinical work suggest that these are the problems you will discover and solve most frequently when you use this book's system for instant stress relief.

For example, let's say your highest score above 66 was on the Stress in Your Mind Scale. When you check your three sources of stress during the day, you will probably find problems with psychological stress more often than from your situation or your body. If your score on the Stress in Your Body Scale was below 66 but higher than your score on the Stress in Your Situation Scale, then you will probably find physical stress more often than situational stress during an average day.

High Levels of Stress

If any of your three stress scale scores was above a percentile rank of 93, then you probably have a problem severe enough to require a stress consultation with a physician or a mental health professional. Additional testing may also be helpful. There is more information about these services in chapters 17, 18, and 37.

If any of your stress scale scores met or exceeded the ninety-eighth percentile, or if the sum of the three percentile ranks on page

63 was greater than 278, then there is a *very* strong probability that you have a significant stress problem which requires professional attention.

Professional Help Is Not for Everyone with High Scores

If you are going through a crisis or a major change in your life, your stress scale scores may be higher than desirable. However, such scores may not indicate the need for professional help. That is particularly true if you know that the period of readjustment will be of fairly short duration.

Our nervous systems and our bodies are well designed for handling short-term, intensive stress. A high score may simply represent such a period of time in your life. If, however, you think the score is fairly representative of your situation over a long period of time or if you have more than one very high score, then a medical or mental health consultation is strongly recommended.

Another way to determine if you need a professional stress consultation is to try the system described in this book for 90 to 120 days, then retake the Seven-Minute Stress Test. If your test scores and the stress symptoms listed in chapter 2 have not decreased, professional consultation would be warranted.

The instant stress relief system is *not a substitute for professional treatment that uses relaxation, biofeedback, or stress-management techniques.* However, our clinical experience suggests that individuals with high stress levels derive great benefit from this system after they have successfully completed treatment.

If You Are Tipping the Scales of Stress . . .

Your stress scores are the keys to understanding your stress load and what to do about it. The higher your scores, the more likely it is that you are suffering from an overload. Being overloaded with stress is like being overweight; the more overweight you are, the more your weight causes you problems.

Let's take this comparison with weight one step further. If you are overweight, chances are your weight problem is caused by one or more of three things: the kinds of foods you eat, the quantity of food you eat, and the amount of exercise you get. You may eat the right kinds of foods but entirely too much of them, and without enough exercise. To control your weight, then, you would keep eating properly—but work on the other two factors as well.

Similarly, after looking at your sources of stress, you can discover which types of coping techniques might best control your problem. To relieve your stress and to reduce your health risk, you will want to practice the techniques that match the stress sources with your highest scores. They are the ones making you heavy with stress and fat with frustration.

With the right stress "diet" and "exercise," you can shed some of your excess stress, and just like the overweight person who loses twenty pounds safely, you will be healthier. Losing those extra "pounds" will also give you a safety zone for managing periods of major stress—and we will all get those once in a while.

9

How Soon Can You Learn to Relieve Your Stress Instantly?

When you become skillful at instant stress relief, you will be able to check all your sources quickly—situation, mind, and body—for distress. Then, by correctly matching the best stress strategy to each problem, you will be able to use the appropriate strategies to achieve maximum results.

Replacing Old Habits

How long does it take to learn these skills? Research by Charles F. Stroebel, M.D., Ph.D., shows that it takes about six months of practice and use for a new stress-management skill to replace an old habit completely.

As you can see from the next figure, after three months, a new skill can be used faster, more effectively, and more automatically than in the first month. The more often you practice a new skill, the sooner it will become part of your life-style.

Beware of impatience. Change takes time. Instant stress relief is a little like "instant printing while you wait." Avoid trying to change too much too quickly and whipping yourself for being a failure. Start with one or two techniques, set realistic goals, and tell yourself, "I'm learning and making progress."

Figure 8: The time it takes for a new skill to become automatic

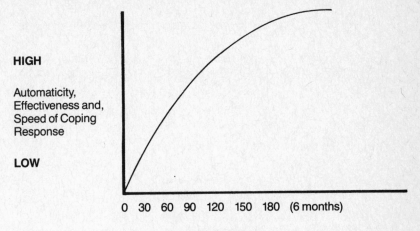

HIGH

Automaticity,
Effectiveness and,
Speed of Coping
Response

LOW

0   30   60   90   120   150   180   (6 months)

DAYS OF PRACTICE

The following story illustrates the way people learn most new skills.

New Habits to the Rescue

During the presidency of Lyndon Johnson, the federal government decided it would start a new program called revenue sharing, under which it would share tax money with local governments.

One day, a small town in New England got a big sum of money from Washington. The citizens did not know quite what to do with the money, so they called a town meeting.

At the meeting, they decided they needed to build a new fire station. To preserve the beauty of the town square, they resolved to add on to the old station and to turn the first floor of the original structure into a fire-fighting museum. The fire fighters would still sleep in the same area over the museum, but another pole would be installed several feet past the old pole to allow quick access to the equipment in the new addition.

What do you suppose happened the first time the bell went off? Most of the fire fighters found themselves sliding down the old pole into the museum! They had to find the door, go outside, and walk around to the new addition to get their modern equipment. When an emergency hit, they automatically followed their old pattern of reacting.

Most people learning the instant stress-relief system have the same problem at first. When an alarm goes off in their lives, they react the old way. When this happens to you, remember the fire fighters. At first, they found themselves all the way down in the museum. Then they caught themselves just going through the floor. Finally, they caught themselves grabbing the old pole and were able to go around to the new pole. It took time, but after a few months, they were automatically sliding down the new pole to their modern equipment.

As you practice instant stress relief, you will have to concentrate on catching yourself when you respond in the old, unhealthy, and unproductive way. At first, like the fire fighters, you will catch yourself too late at times. But as you practice applying the powerful coping strategies in this book, you will quickly and automatically find a way to put yourself back into the optimal stress range.

Relieving
the
Stress
of
Your Body

10

Measuring Your Minute-to-Minute Stress

Listening to Your Body

You may have learned from the list of stress symptoms or the Seven-Minute Stress Test that your body is a major source of your problem. This is useful information, but it is not a minute-to-minute gauge of stress.

To measure your ongoing stress, it is helpful to review the story of the cave dweller and the saber-toothed tiger. When the shadow of the tiger threatened, the cave dweller's muscles tensed up to prepare for fight or flight. This response is why you may feel uptight when you deal with stress.

Remember how blood flowed away from the cave dweller's hands and feet to fuel the large muscles of the upper arms and legs. This loss of blood is why your hands may feel cold when you are under stress.

Use the following techniques to check your muscle tension or your hand temperature.

Scanning for Tension

When you scan, you are checking different muscles in your body as if you could x-ray each part and look for tension.

Start at the top of your head and scan down through your scalp, forehead, and jaw. See if you are clenching your teeth. Check your neck muscles for any tension, tightness, or pain. Scan your shoulder muscles and arms. Check your breathing to see if it is rapid, uneven, and shallow rather than slow, regular, and deep. Scan your upper legs for tightness. See if your calves are tense. Finally, check your toes for curling or pain.

After you have scanned your body for tension, you can quickly check your hand temperature with the quick test on your *pocket guide*.

Your Built-in Stress Test: A Rule of Hand

For those few occasions when you do not have your guide in your pocket or purse, there is another way of telling if your body is under stress. It is not as precise and has the same limitations as the quick test, but it can give you helpful information. Place your hand on the side of your neck just above your collar. If your hand is cooler than your neck, your hand temperature indicates that your body is probably stressed.

Bob, a salesperson who took our workshop, found still another way of using hand temperature. When Bob meets a customer and shakes hands, he pays attention to whose hand is cooler. Unless one of them just came from a cooler place or a more stressful situation, Bob has a good clue as to who may be more anxious about the sale!

Six Quick Ways to Check Your Body's Stress

You now know some instant ways of checking your body for stress. We recommend using a technique to relieve body stress whenever you want to be more productive or relaxed, but particularly under any of the six conditions listed below.

You may need relief from the stress of your body when:

1. You scan and find *muscle tension*
2. You take the *quick test* with your *pocket guide* and find the number of the lowest colored cell is greater than two
3. You check your *hand temperature* and find it cooler than your neck
4. You find yourself *sweating* nervously
5. You check and find a *rapid pulse* of more than seventy-five beats per minute
6. You find your *breathing is shallow* and rapid

You have been learning about the fight-or-flight emergency response as a way of understanding and measuring your stress.

How to deal with it? Start using the "stay-and-play" relaxation response.

11

Training Your Body to Relax

The emergency response and the relaxation response are different parts of our nervous systems. Unfortunately, many people use the fight-or-flight response when the stay-and-play response would be not only healthier but more productive.

Most of today's challenges require calm persistence or creative problem solving. Both are easier to achieve when we are relaxed.

The Many Uses of Relaxation Training in Medicine

Relaxation training is widely used in medicine. It is a recognized treatment alone or in combination with other interventions for headaches, high blood pressure, insomnia, digestive problems, skin problems, and most other stress-related disorders.

Relaxation is so useful and safe that it has been called a "behavioral aspirin." Fewer than four out of every hundred patients in relaxation therapy report any unpleasant side effects.

A few patients report muscle cramps during the tension-release techniques described below. If you avoid tensing cold, tired muscles, especially those in the hands or feet, and you relax in a warm room or cover yourself with a blanket, you are unlikely ever to have a cramp. If you do, simply stretch and knead the cramped muscle.

While most of the medical research about relaxation to date has focused on treatment, more and more studies speak to its value in preventive medicine. Some exciting new research strongly suggests that relaxation may even improve our immunity to disease.

Relaxation and a President's Speech Anxiety

Relaxation may be most useful when you are doing something important, because you want to get the right balance between energy and skill.

The president of a large service organization came to us for greater control over his speech anxiety. He was quite capable of speaking in front of groups or he would not have been asked to lead the organization. His physician had offered him some medication, but the president had refused it because he wanted to use his anxious energy to add fire to parts of his speeches. His goal was to optimize his performance.

As he learned the relaxation techniques that you will be learning, he found that he was able to remember the contents of his speeches better, deal more creatively with the unexpected, and communicate with far greater effectiveness.

The power of his convictions was conveyed, but rather than being almost overwhelmed by anxiety, he became comfortable enough with speaking that he even began experimenting with humor. Most importantly, he began to enjoy an activity that had made him very anxious in the past.

Our work teaches us many things. Some of the most effective techniques are simple and short. The speech-anxious president found the breathing exercises below of immediate help and of much more value than we would have predicted. We now know that changing one's breathing pattern is the first step toward instant stress relief for many people.

Breathing Stress Away

When you find muscle tension, cool hands, nervous sweating, irregular breathing, or a rapid pulse, one of the best ways to restore relaxation is to change the way you are breathing.

Your lungs are the carburetors of your body's engine. Breathing increases the oxygen level in your bloodstream and sets the tone of many stress reactions in your body.

Under stress, many people tend to breathe from their middle chests in a somewhat rapid and very shallow way. This may have evolved to accommodate short bursts of running or fighting, but it is not a comfortable, long-term solution. Research suggests it can also lead to high blood pressure.

The following exercise can help you breathe stress away. Before you begin, scan your muscles for tension and use the *pocket guide*'s quick test for temperature. After the exercise, you can check again to see how well you have been able to relax.

Deep-Breathing Technique

Breathe in slowly through your nose as you count up to five: "In, 1, 2, 3, 4, 5."

For the best results, fill your stomach area first. Push it out and let it expand. After you fill the lower parts of your lungs, let your chest rise up and out until the upper parts are filled.

Leave about a second between each number. At the count of five, your lungs should be nearly full and you should be unable to breathe in any more air comfortably.

After a full inspiration, slowly release the air out through your nose or mouth, counting backward, "Out, 5, 4, 3, 2, 1." Be sure you empty your lungs almost entirely.

To complete this relaxation exercise, take two more of these deep, satisfying breaths.

Now, recheck your muscle tension and hand temperature. If you find little or no change, you may want to repeat the exercise before trying the additional techniques below.

With practice, checking for stress before and after the technique will take about half a minute. Figure another half minute for deep breathing and you have a surprisingly effective, one-minute technique for stress relief. Once you have used this one-minute technique several times, you may wish to shorten it and see if it is still of benefit. Some people are able to scan for tension as they breathe in, and relax as they slowly breathe out. It is a lot like a silent sigh of relaxation.

There are many ways of doing the deep-breathing technique. For example, some people add a little more rhythm by counting, "In, 2, 3, 4, 5 . . . Out, 2, 3, 4, 5." Others start with the exhale, "Out, 5, 4, 3, 2, 1," and hold it until it becomes uncomfortable. When they finally breathe in, it brings a wonderful sense of relief. Others focus on the cool air flowing into their noses and the warm air flowing back out again. Each of the three authors of this book uses a somewhat different breathing technique. Experiment and find the one that works best for you.

Sometimes, we call the deep-breathing technique "belly breathing." This helps people smile and remember to breathe deeply.

People who are shallow breathers or heavy cigarette smokers may feel a little lightheaded after a lengthy deep-breathing exercise. This lightheadedness comes because more oxygen is getting to the brain. Most of the time, the feeling is just a comfortable, settling sensation—something to enjoy as your deep breathing naturally relaxes your body.

The next time you feel rushed or upset, breathe slowly and deeply. It takes very little effort and yields many rewards. You can even do this exercise while you walk. Breathe in as you count four steps, out as you count the next four, and repeat as needed.

Is your speech explosive or pressured? You may be increasing your risk of high blood pressure. Consider honoring the commas and periods in your speech. Pauses give you time to breathe deeper.

The deep-breathing technique can also be combined with muscle relaxation by letting go of every muscle sequentially from the top of your head to the tips of your toes as you exhale each breath.

The next section will help you learn much more about muscle relaxation. However, if you have not yet tried the deep-breathing technique, we want to encourage you to do so now.

Tensing Stress Away

Following are two major ways of relaxing your muscles. The first, involving tensing and then releasing the muscles in your body, was discovered by a physician named Edmund Jacobson. Dr. Jacobson found that people could relax a muscle to a significantly greater degree *after* tensing it than before. The second technique is called "recall relaxation," and we'll deal with it in the next chapter.

The tension-release technique can help you become more aware of the muscles in your body and of the differences between muscle tension and relaxation. After repeated practice with the technique, most people can learn to get much the same effect by just releasing their muscles. When you are learning the technique, however, you can tense and release your muscles in the following way. The first few times, we recommend finding a quiet place where you can lie down, loosen any tight clothing, and remove your shoes.

Before you try this exercise, scan your muscle tension and either place your hand on the side of your neck or use the *pocket guide*'s quick test. Later you can check your progress.

Whenever you use this or any other relaxation technique, be sure to continue breathing slowly from your stomach area in deep, satisfying breaths.

The Tension-and-Release Technique

Squint your eyes and grit your teeth together. Hold this muscle tension for about five seconds and then let it go. Feel the warmth of relaxation flowing into the muscles as the tension leaves.

Leaving your facial muscles relaxed, tilt your head back and draw up your shoulders as if you were trying to touch your ears with your shoulders. Tighten your stomach muscles as if someone were about to punch you in the stomach. Study all this tension for about five seconds, then let it go. Feel the relaxation and perhaps some warmth and heaviness flowing into your neck, shoulders, and stomach.

Leaving your other muscles relaxed, make a fist with each hand and make a muscle in each upper arm as if you were weight lifting. Hold it, study the tension for about five seconds, and then let go. You may feel some pleasant warmth or tingling, heaviness, or lightness as the blood flow increases in your arms and hands.

Next, keep all the previously tensed muscles totally relaxed, but squeeze your buttocks, tighten your upper and lower legs, and curl your feet and toes. Study the tension for about five seconds, then let it go. Feel the warmth, heaviness, and relaxation flow into all your muscles and a comfortable, calm feeling spread throughout your body.

Become more and more alert mentally, but let your body remain relaxed. You will feel like you just woke up from a refreshing nap.

After you complete the relaxation exercise, scan your body for tension and check your hand temperature. Usually, the change in muscle tension is more noticeable than the change in hand temperature.

If your muscle tension is the same or if your temperature is not in the "partly relaxed" to "very relaxed" range on the *pocket guide*, then you may want to repeat the exercise. You may also want to lengthen the exercise by adding muscles or breaking the muscle groups into their components and tensing each of them for five seconds. For example, squint your eyes, release; then grit your teeth, release; and so on.

If you find your hand temperature is repeatedly the same or even decreases, don't get discouraged. The techniques in the next chapter have more impact on blood flow, and thus on hand temperature, than the ones presented in this chapter.

Taped Relaxation Training

Many people find reading step-by-step directions for the tension and release technique difficult or distracting while they are learning to relax.

You may want to read the directions into a tape recorder using a slow, deep voice while playing your favorite instrumental music as background. There are also many relaxation tapes available commercially. Some of the better ones are listed in the last chapter of this book.

12

Using Recall Relaxation

In the last chapter, you learned about the tension-release technique. After you have used that technique several times, perhaps once or twice a day for a week, you may want to try recall relaxation.

Direct your attention to the same muscle groups as in the tension-and-release technique, but ignore the instructions to tense. Simply recall what your muscles felt like just after you released the tension. As you slowly tour your body, gently let go of every muscle.

Deepening Recall Relaxation

To deepen this relaxation, you may want to find the most relaxed part of your body and slowly allow this relaxation to spread in gentle waves to the rest of your body.

Another deepening technique involves counting backward slowly from ten to one. You allow yourself to become more and more relaxed as you count down each of the numbers, or each of the ten floors on an imaginary elevator or each step on a spiral staircase in your mind.

Adding a Cue Word

Once you have deepened this relaxation, silently repeat a relaxing word or phrase in the back of your mind. Many people use *relax*, *calm*, or *day off*. Let the word you choose echo in your mind.

After repeatedly associating this word or phrase with deep relaxation, it will become a cue or signal for your body to relax. You can start using it in mildly stressful situations to recall rapidly the feelings of deep relaxation.

During relaxation practice, most people find their minds wander. Just let the thoughts leave as easily and quickly as they came. You may find it helpful to imagine your thoughts as soap bubbles, floating up and out of your mind. Then gently return to your relaxation and repeat your cue word.

Tape Recording Your Favorite Sounds

You may also want to make or buy a tape for recall relaxation. It is fun to add not only instrumental music but also environmental sounds.

Try taping waves lapping against the shore, crickets chirping in the night, or rain dancing on a metal roof. Maybe you would prefer taping late-night city sounds—whatever you find most relaxing. You could even use several machines to play your favorite backgrounds as you record the relaxation instructions.

At first, with or without a tape, it may be best to relax in a quiet place alone. With practice, you will be able to use your cue word to relax instantly, anywhere and at any time.

Using a Six-Second Tranquilizer

Some people call brief periods of recall relaxation "six-second tranquilizers." After enough practice, it only takes about six seconds to feel a pleasant sense of relaxation spreading over your body.

One of the problems with other forms of relaxation is the amount of time they take. Most people do not have the time or discipline to practice a relaxation technique twenty minutes, twice a day, for the rest of their lives.

84

With a six-second tranquilizer, you have plenty of time. The average American spends forty minutes a day waiting. If you are like most people, you wait for stop signs, elevators, cashiers, and meetings. You are placed on hold and sit through hours of dull commercials each week. You can wait impatiently and stressfully, or you can take an instant to enjoy a health-enhancing relaxation break.

Busy parents who carpool can practice relaxation while waiting for children. Commuters who wait for taxis and airplanes may want to use those times to relax.

Answering the Telephone in a New Way

When the telephone rings, you can dive for it angrily or you can wait two rings and give yourself an instant tranquilizer. People who use this new way of answering the telephone find they are more calm, confident, and competent because they feel in control and they begin their conversations in a relaxed state.

It is important to find many cues or signals in your daily routine to remind you to relax.

Do you check your watch many times a day? You might put a piece of colored tape on it as a signal to relax. Or, whenever you sit down, you might let your muscles melt and your breathing deepen. Be creative and find both cues and time for your relaxation.

A Busy Executive Squeaks No More

Joan, a busy executive we treated successfully for headaches, learned to use cue-controlled relaxation and reported two unexpected benefits.

Whenever Joan was tempted to interrupt someone, she used the situation as a cue to relax. Joan discovered she heard more of what was said, and her communications with others improved. In addition, Joan found that she no longer "squeaked." Joan's relaxed breathing lowered her voice and added authority to her words. Overall, Joan said, "I still get rushed, but not upset."

Combining Relaxation Techniques

Once you have learned some relaxation techniques, you may want to try combining them. For example, you might combine scanning for tension with recall relaxation in the following way.

Scan a section of your body for tension. Then, recalling how it felt right after you let go of the tension using the tension-release technique, allow the section to relax. Move on to the next section of your body, scan, and let go.

You may want to scan and relax every section of your body or just the ones where you carry tension. The muscles of the shoulders and stomach are two of the most common sites.

The long or short forms of these techniques, plus the ones in the next chapter and their various combinations, can be used in many situations, depending on your skill.

Red-Light Relaxation

A workshop participant who had always raced dangerously through red lights or fumed when he waited for them to turn green decided to use the time for a sixty-second sedative.

The participant chose to combine scanning for tension and recalling deep relaxation while he enjoyed the music on his cassette player. He told us later that he stopped speeding through intersections and now looked forward to what he called his "red-light relaxation."

Your Initial Investment

Our emphasis on brief techniques is supported not only by the success achieved by our patients and workshop participants but also by a number of studies here and abroad.

A British medical team headed by Dr. Chandra Patel reported such a study in 1985. Four years after an eight-hour relaxation and stress-management course, eighty-one people with above-average coronary risk had fewer coronary incidents and maintained lower average blood pressure and cholesterol levels than a control group.

Only fourteen of those who took the course were still practicing formal relaxation regularly, but sixty-six said they sometimes used it in their everyday life. These results suggest that brief forms of relaxation may be very important for long-term stress relief.

The tension-and-release technique requires more privacy and time than the brief relaxation techniques in this chapter, but consider it as your initial investment. If you put in the time, you will be able to use the shorter relaxation skills to enhance your health for the rest of your life.

13

Using Biofeedback

Follow the directions on your *pocket guide* or in the beginning of this book to position your fingers for biofeedback and to read your initial temperature. Then record the temperature in the "before" box on the chart at the end of the book.

To start temperature biofeedback, use deep breathing and recall relaxation. Keep your eyes open and continue relaxing. Imagine yourself in a place where you are very warm, comfortable, and relaxed. Allow the warmth to flow into your hands.

Many different mental and sensory strategies can produce a biofeedback-assisted relaxation response. The goal is to send a "relax" signal to the nerves that control the tension levels of the blood vessels in the hands and feet. When the vessels relax, more warm blood flows into the fingers and toes.

As your hands warm up, your blood pressure goes down in a healthy way. The relaxation brings relief throughout your body.

Of Beaches, Mountain Cabins, and Hot Tubs

Some people find it useful to imagine themselves on a beautiful summer day, lying on a beach, taking in the warm rays of the sun. They imagine sliding their hands under the warm sand and feeling the pleasant warmth flow through their fingers.

Other people imagine lying in a hot tub and being massaged by warm water. The water and warmth pulsate through every cell of their bodies.

For quick reference, these images are briefly described in a paragraph of blue type in the directions for biofeedback on your *pocket guide*.

Some people prefer to imagine sitting in front of a fireplace in a mountain cabin during the wintertime. They stretch out their hands to enjoy fully the warmth of the roaring fire. The light and heat bounce onto their hands, warming them to the core.

Still other people imagine sitting in front of a window and feeling the heat of the sun by pressing their fingers against the windowpane. Any image that increases blood flow and warmth may be used to relax during biofeedback.

Hitting the Nail in Your Head

Not everyone has a vivid imagination for visualizing. The following is an exercise we have used successfully many times with people who have difficulty imagining the scenes just described.

We ask them to make believe that they have hit their fingertip with a hammer and can feel the throbbing and pulsing of blood in their fingertip. But we ask them to do so without feeling any pain. Their hands begin to warm—a sign that they are relaxing. Even if you have a good imagination, you may find this a useful technique.

These hand-warming exercises can be used for any length of time—from a few seconds to thirty minutes—depending on your schedule and on the amount of tension in your nervous system.

You will know if your nervous system is relaxing or getting more tense by watching the lowest-numbered sensor square. For the best feedback, reposition the pad of your finger under that particular square. Watch it change hue as shown on the color strip. It can change from tense brown or tan to partly relaxed green or turquoise and then to relaxed blue or violet.

How Far Can You Go?

If there is a good deal of stress and tension in your nervous system when you start an exercise, then you may go through several of these changes in hue. Each square has a temperature range of five degrees. First, you may see the colors change on the sensor square where you started and then begin to show up on a square with a lower number as you continue to relax.

The more stressed you are before your biofeedback session and the colder your hands when you start, the more range you have to increase your blood flow and finger temperature.

With practice and a cold start, some people can go through two or even three different squares, increasing their finger temperature ten or more degrees!

What If the Temperature Goes Down Instead of Up?

When you are just starting to learn biofeedback, it is very common for changes in color and even in square number to indicate a decrease in temperature.

Sometimes, changes in hand temperature may result from changes in room temperature. You may want to check the thermostat and look for an air-conditioning duct that could be blowing cold air on your hands. However, a far more common explanation involves the frustration and stress that come from trying too hard.

When you try too hard, you trigger the fight-or-flight response rather than the relaxation response. Blood flows away from the hands rather than to them, and your hands become colder.

If your temperature goes down, don't get discouraged. At least you know that you can change your hand temperature. Now, it is time to find a different approach to raise the temperature.

90

Trying Not to Try

If you successfully raised your hand temperature, the following information may help you to do even better. If your hand temperature stayed the same or went down, this section could be all you need to start getting great results.

When you do biofeedback, a stay-and-play approach works far better than a serious, do-or-die approach. Worrying about your performance only undermines your efforts. This process has also been called "persistent noneffort."

To relax deeply, you actually need to try *not* to try.

Trying not to try is a difficult process to describe. Some have called it "passive concentration," which means you just enrich your mental images until you can sense your pulse throbbing in your fingertips.

No one can force you to relax. It is not something even *you* can force yourself to do. You cannot command your body to relax; it only relaxes if you are open and receptive to relaxation. Relaxation is something you must allow to happen.

For many people, relaxation is a difficult skill to learn because they have been taught that nothing of value is ever achieved without effort. While this idea is true even in biofeedback, the effort here involves putting aside time on a regular basis to experiment with and to explore this new mode of experience.

Be patient with yourself and avoid learning fatigue. Keep practice sessions shorter than thirty minutes.

The End of a Session

When you have decided to terminate your biofeedback session, check the color and hue of the lowest-numbered sensor square and look up your exact temperature on the chart above the color strip of your *pocket guide*. Then, enter the temperature in the "after" space on your biofeedback practice chart at the end of this book.

If the temperature has gone up and the room temperature is the same, then you have brought about the desired effect. Congratulations! If the temperature has gone down, you may want to reread the last few pages for an explanation and additional help.

With practice, you may want to become aware of the subtle feelings you experience when you are succeeding at biofeedback. Some feel a pulsing sensation; others, a tingling feeling. Still others feel heaviness or lightness as the blood flows into their hands and feet. You can use these subtle feelings as signals of success when you decide not to use your *pocket guide*.

Other Uses of Temperature Biofeedback

You may be interested in some of the many ways temperature biofeedback is used in medical and industrial settings. Patients with Raynaud's disease, for instance, have cold, painful hands and feet. Many can be taught to control their symptoms by using biofeedback alone or in combination with medication.

Migraine headache sufferers are also treated with biofeedback. When the blood vessels in their heads constrict, some experience a visual aura or other warning signs. If they use the signs as cues and dilate those blood vessels by warming their hands, they can usually abort the headache.

Over time, many migraine sufferers manage their stress well enough to avoid even the early symptoms. One of our migraine patients uses the *pocket guide* every few hours to keep his hands above 90 degrees F and out of what he calls "headache territory."

People who work in cold temperatures can also use thermal biofeedback to warm their hands. It has been used indoors by butchers in meat-packing plants, for example, and outdoors by construction workers in Alaska.

With warmer hands, people in these jobs can work comfortably for longer periods of time. They can also better manipulate objects with their fingers since they can wear gloves rather than mittens.

More About Your *Pocket Guide*

Your guide's microencapsulated liquid cholesteric sensor cells are as impressive as their name suggests. If you use the shades of color on the strip below the temperature chart on your *pocket guide*, you can read the square cells to within one-half a degree accuracy. This degree of sensitivity has been shown to be optimal for learning the hand-warming response with such crystal cells.

Now that you have learned the instant stress relief skills for the body, you can use the guide in several ways. You can take the quick test for stress or use the color strip for a more accurate check. If you have a little more time, you can take a biofeedback break instead of a coffee break.

On the inside panel of the *pocket guide*, you will find a brief description of an instant, three-step technique for handling your body's stress. This technique combines some of the major forms of relaxation you have learned, in a way many people find helpful. Figure 9 highlights this section of the panel.

The guide has been designed to fit easily into your pocket or purse. We recommend that you carry it as a reminder to relieve your stress and to enhance your health throughout the day.

How to Care for Your *Pocket Guide*

Your *pocket guide* is made of durable materials, but experience suggests that you should avoid exposing it to extreme temperatures. Leaving it in a car, say, during a blizzard or a heat wave will destroy the liquid crystals in the sensor.

Accidentally dry cleaning or machine washing the *pocket guide* will loosen the bond between the sensor square and the cardboard. That may also happen if you sit on the guide, bend it too much, or use excessive pressure during repeated biofeedback. If the sensor loosens, simply reglue it to the cardboard with fast-drying glue.

Additional *Pocket Guides*

If you damage your *pocket guide*, lose it, or want to get one for a friend, additional cards are available for $3.95 each. Send a check or money order made out to DPC, Inc., along with a self-addressed, stamped envelope to 3300 Virginia Avenue, #2, Shreveport, Louisiana 71103. Please allow up to four weeks for delivery. Quantity discounts are also available.

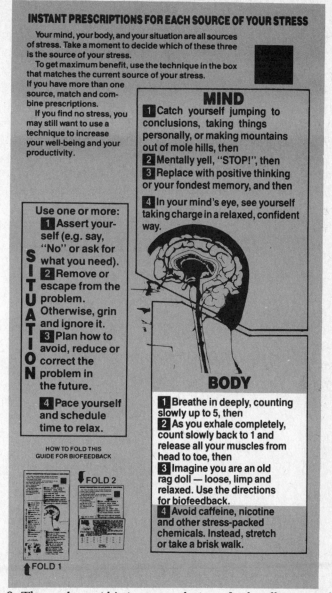

INSTANT PRESCRIPTIONS FOR EACH SOURCE OF YOUR STRESS

Your mind, your body, and your situation are all sources of stress. Take a moment to decide which of these three is the source of your stress.

To get maximum benefit, use the technique in the box that matches the current source of your stress.

If you have more than one source, match and combine prescriptions.

If you find no stress, you may still want to use a technique to increase your well-being and your productivity.

MIND

1. Catch yourself jumping to conclusions, taking things personally, or making mountains out of mole hills, then
2. Mentally yell, "STOP!", then
3. Replace with positive thinking or your fondest memory, and then
4. In your mind's eye, see yourself taking charge in a relaxed, confident way.

SITUATION

Use one or more:
1. Assert yourself (e.g. say, "No" or ask for what you need).
2. Remove or escape from the problem. Otherwise, grin and ignore it.
3. Plan how to avoid, reduce or correct the problem in the future.
4. Pace yourself and schedule time to relax.

HOW TO FOLD THIS GUIDE FOR BIOFEEDBACK

FOLD 2

FOLD 1

BODY

1. Breathe in deeply, counting slowly up to 5, then
2. As you exhale completely, count slowly back to 1 and release all your muscles from head to toe, then
3. Imagine you are an old rag doll — loose, limp and relaxed. Use the directions for biofeedback.
4. Avoid caffeine, nicotine and other stress-packed chemicals. Instead, stretch or take a brisk walk.

Figure 9: The *pocket guide*'s instant technique for handling your body's stress

Other Forms of Biofeedback

Your *pocket guide*, with its half-degree accuracy, may be the best biofeedback card of its kind. However, most thermal biofeedback instruments used in clinical practice are electronic and offer accuracy down to a tenth of a degree. In addition, other electronic instruments can provide information about different parts of your body's response to stress.

If you are unable to raise your hand temperature into the relaxed range after considerable practice with your biofeedback guide, then you may wish to seek electronic biofeedback training from a therapist in your area. More information about biofeedback specialists is in the last chapter of this book.

14

Body Building for Stress Management

S tudies of healthy people have repeatedly pointed to exercise, weight control, and other body-building activities as ways to beat the odds on disease, disability, and early death. You may be familiar with some of these findings, but you may not know how these activities can help you relieve your body's stress.

Even if you understand the stress connections, knowing what to do and doing it regularly are two very different things. Here is where instant stress relief can make all the difference.

Some of the suggestions that follow in this and the next chapter take more than an instant. However, they may take less time than you think and should help you take the healthiest turns at the moments when you face the daily decisions of living.

We hope you will be surprised by how many of the suggestions are small, take only a few minutes, and yet deliver major, long-lasting benefits.

Fight or Flight in Modern Life

Exercising the legs, arms, heart, and lungs by walking, running, or engaging in other vigorous activity is the closest thing to regular fight or flight in modern life.

Exercise burns off the biochemical byproducts of the stress response; it is one of nature's best tranquilizers. Studies have also shown that regular exercise reduces hostility by as much as 60 percent and depression by as much as 30 percent among healthy adults. Those who exercise also report less constipation and more restful sleep.

For many years, it was difficult to find conclusive evidence that exercise could prolong life. However, a very convincing study of nearly seventeen thousand men who entered college from 1916 to 1950 was recently published in the *New England Journal of Medicine*. In a *Time* interview, the principal author of the study summarized the findings in a most encouraging way, "For each hour of physical activity, you can expect to live that hour over—and live one or two more hours to boot."

The same study showed that, even if you don't start until you are an adult, exercise can increase your life expectancy. However, if you are starting an exercise program and you are thirty-five years or older, check with your physician first. In addition, it is important to avoid what some researchers have called the four-day phenomenon.

The Four-Day Phenomenon

Most of us can diet to starvation and exercise to exhaustion for about four days. Then we give up until the next time we are encouraged to begin dieting or exercising. These short, intense bursts are a major strain on the body, particularly the heart.

If you insist on straining your body and on inviting injury, it might be healthier to imitate W. C. Fields: "Whenever the urge to exercise comes over me, I lie down and wait for it to pass."

The Best Physical Exercise Takes More Than an Instant

It is best to develop a regular vigorous activity or sport that uses the large muscle groups gradually. Here, there are no instant solutions. However, an aerobics program—the kind that many believe to be the best physical exercise—requires very little time.

Only a half-hour, three or four times a week, is needed for an aerobics program—less than 2 percent of your waking hours. Furthermore, for each minute devoted to exercise, you can expect a two- or three-minute return on your investment.

Dr. Kenneth Cooper is acknowledged as the pioneering researcher on aerobics. Dr. Cooper has shown that cardiac fitness is conditioned by working the heart at rates that are challenging but still safe.

If you are healthy, you can use the chart in figure 10 to find your target heart-rate zone. By maintaining your pulse in this zone during regular exercise or play, you should safely achieve cardiorespiratory fitness.

These rates were calculated from the recommendations given by Kenneth H. Cooper, M.D., for women and unfit men in his *Running Without Fear* (New York: Evans, 1985). To compute these rates, subtract your age from 220 and multiply the resulting figure by .65 (for the lower rate) and by .80 (for the higher rate). Men who have been exercising regularly may instead begin by subtracting *half* their ages from 205 and multiplying by .65 and .80.

If you are just starting an aerobics program, we cannot overemphasize the importance of small, slow increments. Muscle pain often occurs because your body's ability to use oxygen is better than your muscle tone. That is why you may tend to overwork your muscles before you are winded. This pain is not necessary to achieve aerobic fitness and can be avoided by increasing your workout gradually.

You are probably not trying to become an Olympic athlete or a model, so give up the old saying, "No pain, no gain." Your new goal is energizing aerobic training, free of both pain and strain.

Aerobic dancing is popular, but one survey found one of three dancers had sustained high-impact injuries. The newer "soft" aerobics, in which you keep one foot on the floor at all times, and water aerobics are safer alternatives. In addition, if you have a "winning-

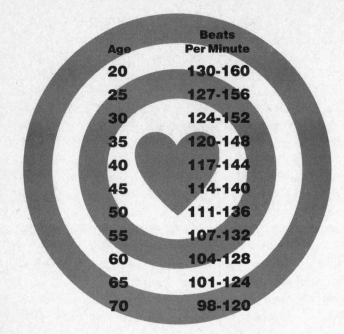

Age	Beats Per Minute
20	130-160
25	127-156
30	124-152
35	120-148
40	117-144
45	114-140
50	111-136
55	107-132
60	104-128
65	101-124
70	98-120

Figure 10: Target heart-rate zone for aerobic training by age

is-everything" attitude, it may be best to avoid the physical and emotional stress of competitive sports.

Whatever exercise you choose, be sure to stretch and to warm up before you start each session. Recent research also emphasizes the importance of a few minutes of walking to cool down and prevent a post-workout heart attack.

Fun and Convenient

Research has shown that you cannot store the physical or the psychological benefits of exercise. If you are going to exercise regularly for the rest of your life, it has to be fun, convenient, and safe.

That may be why research has also shown that if you start by walking rather than jogging, you will be more likely to be exercising a year later. To make the exercise more fun, try to find a companion—be it a friend, a pet, or even a portable cassette player.

If your spouse walks too slowly to be a good exercise partner, try wearing a six-pound backpack. The pack distributes the added weight without tying up your hands. If you add weight gradually, the pack can increase your heart rate up to your target zone.

You may want to leave a pair of sneakers at work and take an energizing walk or run during your lunch hour. If you travel by plane, airports offer miles of walkways for the time you have between flights. Shopping malls can be used as indoor walking facilities. If you go to a mall in the early morning hours, you are likely to find lots of company.

Investing in Your Fitness

Consider making an investment in your physical fitness. Many people join fitness centers or spas; and while such clubs work well for some people, research shows that most new members will go five or fewer times.

If fitness facilities are not for you, consider investing the cost of membership in your own exercise equipment. We recommend buying the best you can afford.

If you do buy or own equipment, you might want to keep track of how often you use the machine and divide the cost by your use. You'll be aware of the current price of each walk, ride, or row— which should evoke some motivating guilt. Each time you use the equipment you will be rewarded by knowing you have reduced the cost per use. It is a little like paying off a loan, but this is a loan with lifelong benefits.

Maintaining Your Motivation

As you slowly increase your aerobics activity, make it pleasant and reward yourself. If you decide to ride a stationary bicycle, for example, you may want to listen to some upbeat music or to wheel it out in front of the TV and schedule rides during your favorite shows.

Let's say you would prefer not to watch the shows while cycling but still want to motivate yourself to stick with your aerobics program. Consider the following approach.

One of the authors found three weekly TV shows he wanted to watch and decided to complete his aerobic exercise before watching them. To keep himself honest and fit, he rides during the programs if he has not exercised before the shows.

You may also want to reward your progress and perseverance with additional sporting equipment, clothing, or other extras. The author who cycles bought a pulse meter after two months and 225 miles. When he lost interest in one of the television programs, he decided to reward himself with a reading stand after another three months and 350 miles.

Another way to maintain motivation is to keep records of time spent or distance moved. For example, you might find an interesting map and use a bright marking pen to show your imaginary cross-country progress.

The Many Benefits of Variety

If you get bored, add variety to your program. Try different activities that exercise the large muscle groups. Consider elevating housework or yard work to an aerobic activity by wearing a light backpack.

To ensure regular workouts, do something aerobic every other day. If you have not found an alternative aerobics activity by the third day, do your regular workout.

Variety can also help those who want to exercise more frequently to lose weight or get in shape faster. By alternating activities, you avoid stressing the same muscle groups on consecutive days.

Variety is also important if an injury keeps you from your regular form of exercise. Swimming is one of the best substitutes when suffering from joint or muscle injuries. If a safe alternative cannot be found, however, resist returning to exercise before your injury heals. Starting back too soon is one of the most common causes of serious injury.

A Few Minutes Here and There

It is also helpful to integrate more physical activity into everyday living. For example, use the stairs instead of the elevator, take a walk instead of a coffee break, and park a little farther from your destination to build in exercise.

Want a reserved parking space where you work or shop? Pick out the last space in the farthest corner of the parking lot. In addition to burning off stress and a few calories every working day, you could avoid all the stress of finding a place to park.

15

Stress in, Stress out

There are a number of chemicals that virtually trigger the stress response. These include caffeine, nicotine, salt, and sugars. Fats and other substances we take into our bodies can put stress on our hearts and on other vital organs. Of the ten major causes of death in America, six are linked to what we eat and drink.

In many ways, what we put in determines what we get out of our bodies. If you know what your goals are, it takes only an instant to choose what you put in—but the right choices can pay years of dividends.

The advice that follows applies to most Americans, but you may need to consult your doctor to see what is best for you. Even if you are familiar with many of these healthy habits, our goal is to present something new that will help you follow each recommendation.

Change is inherently stressful and gradual changes are the longest lasting, so change slowly but persistently.

A Dozen Dietary Steps to Stress Relief

1. Eat three meals a day, especially breakfast. In one study of industrial accidents, 75 percent involved workers who had skipped breakfast.

If it is difficult to schedule three well-balanced meals, avoid becoming a "junk food junkie" and make arrangements to eat one square meal per day. However you like to eat, be sure to include some food from each of the major food groups every day.

If you eat a wide variety of foods, your body will get more of what it needs. In addition, should something you're eating make the cancer-causing list, you'll suffer less stress by knowing you aren't eating huge quantities of it.

2. Take a high-quality vitamin/mineral supplement every day. It should be heavy in vitamin C, the B-complex vitamins, and calcium, but no more than 150 percent of the U.S. Recommended Daily Allowance (RDA). Vitamin C must be absorbed daily because the body cannot store it. If you drink alcohol, be sure to replace the B Complex vitamins it destroys. Calcium is a key factor in stress relief because your muscles use it to relax.

Consider steaming or microwaving your food to help preserve nutrients. In addition, if you eat out more than once a day, your diet is likely to lack vitamin C and calcium. You may want to increase these nutrients by ordering milk or juice.

3. Eat more fiber or what grandma used to call roughage. Fiber is good for cancer prevention, cholesterol reduction, and weight control. A high-fiber diet not only gives you a full feeling, but it decreases caloric absorption by about 10 percent. Consider substituting fresh fruits for juices, but drink more water and add fiber slowly; otherwise, indigestion can result.

4. Limit the cholesterols and saturated fats in your diet. One study of physicians showed that slim doctors carefully avoided food containing solid fat and cut away the visible fat on the few meats they did eat.

The typical American diet contains 40 percent fat. Limit fatty foods, so that no more than 30 percent of your diet is fat and preferably as little as 15 percent. Several studies show blood pressure can be lowered by reducing fat to less than 25 percent.

The best time to trim fat is before you cook it so the meat absorbs less. Avoid fried foods, use low-fat meat and dairy products, and eat smaller portions of foods high in fat.

5. Do not salt your food. Almost all processed foods contain salt, so no additional salt is needed. Research with animals suggests that salt may be a stress-inducing chemical. Salt increases the number of brain-cell receptors for the stress-triggering hormones and seems to promote irritability.

The chemical part of the stress response that sustains alertness in times of uncertainty also makes the body stockpile salt. So, stress may cause more salt to be retained, which in turn may make the body more responsive to stress chemicals. The role of salt in high blood pressure is controversial, but moderation seems best until more is known.

Because salt stimulates the appetite, salt reduction can also help you control your weight. We recommend cutting down slowly. Those who do cut down report that it is a lot easier than giving up cigarettes. After a few weeks, many actually dislike the taste of salt.

Watch out for the leading sources of salt for most Americans: breads; crackers; and processed meats, soups, and cheeses. Also, avoid TV dinners—many have more sodium than you need for a full day's supply. Rinsing some other foods in tap water will help.

You may also want to substitute herbs and spices for salt. Use garlic and onion freely, as well as wine, vinegar, and lemons.

6. Avoid foods containing refined sugar. Substitute more complex carbohydrates such as pasta, bread, and cereal. Sugar is released during the stress response, but the temporary lift it gives you will be followed about one to two hours later by chemically induced weakness and fatigue. Some people misinterpret these feelings as depression. Many only compound the problem with more sugar or caffeine.

Sugar also causes cavities. If you quit smoking and substitute hard candy, be sure you use the sugarless suckers or brush your teeth afterward.

Dental care is stressful for many. It, too, can be relieved with relaxation techniques—imagine that the overhead light is the sun and go to the beach in your mind—but it is far better to prevent dental problems. To make flossing a more regular habit, try doing it while you watch bedtime television.

7. **Know which foods relax you.** Carbohydrates release a sleep-inducing brain chemical called serotonin. Adjusting the balance of carbohydrates to proteins can help you prepare for sleep or work. The calories in a lunch designed for alertness, for example, might be one-third lean meat and two-thirds bread, fruit, and vegetables.

8. **If you drink alcohol, do so in moderation.** Moderate drinking is statistically associated with fewer heart attacks. However, recent research suggests that even light drinkers have more than double the risk of stroke that nondrinkers do. The data is not all in, but too much drinking clearly leads to disease, death, and family disintegration. Alcohol contributes to half the homicides and half the suicides in this country.

If you have gotten in legal, marital, or occupational trouble more than once because of alcohol, you are probably an alcoholic. Get help. Treatment is more effective than ever before.

Don't drink and drive. Driving when intoxicated is the number-three cause of death in this country. Decide early in the evening who is going to stay sober and drive everyone home.

9. **Eat more fish.** Eating fish may help you cut down on unhealthy fats and increase your intake of heart-protective oils. Several studies support this advice. One showed that Dutch men averaging seven ounces of fish per week had only half the rate of coronary disease of those who ate no fish. But be careful—large amounts of fish oil supplements may interfere with blood clotting when you are injured.

10. **If you smoke, stop.** If you cannot stop on your own, get help. Nicotine is a very powerful and fast-acting drug with two dose-dependent effects. Research suggests short, quick puffs trigger an alerting response that is very similar to the fight-or-flight response. Slow, deep drags bring in more nicotine, which stimulates and then soothes. It is difficult to give up a drug that offers a two-way fix.

Smoking is the number-one preventable cause of death in this country; we urge you to stop. It takes as little as two years for an ex-smoker to reduce his threefold greater risk of nonfatal heart attack to about the level of those who have never smoked.

Smoking may also be hazardous to your wealth. One study showed that 46 percent of vice presidents and personnel directors would hire a nonsmoker over an equally qualified smoker. Only 3 percent would prefer the smoker. Part of the reason may be the much higher rates of absenteeism among smokers.

Knowing the two-way fix of nicotine, you may want to *use* the urge to smoke as a cuc for a quick six-second tranquilizer. If you need more energy, find a way to get more sleep.

Research shows those who have tried to quit before are more likely to succeed on their next attempt than first-time quitters. So try, try again until you join the more than 33 million people who have quit smoking in recent years.

11. Monitor your use of caffeine and decrease if indicated. Coffee, tea, and colas are the most popular drinks in America, so caffeine is our most widely used drug. Too much caffeine is stress inducing and can cause nervousness, insomnia, irregular heartbeats, and headaches.

How much is too much? Some have symptoms with as little as two cups of coffee a day, while others can handle six. Your tolerance increases with your weight but decreases with age.

Instant coffee can bring some relief, since it has about two-thirds the caffeine found in brewed coffee; but, of all the coffees, decaffeinated brings the best relief.

The need for the quick stimulation caffeine provides can be met in a number of ways. When listening to a speaker, challenge yourself to imagine what you would present about the topic if you were asked to speak without preparation. Become more curious by asking yourself specifically what you want to learn about the topic. Stimulating your mind will keep you alert and increase retention.

You can also create a certain amount of stimulation and arousal in most situations by exaggerating any possible danger, however remote. Brief naps are another alternative to stimulants. In addition, there are biofeedback devices that hook over your ear and set off an alarm if your head tilts forward.

If you stop caffeine abruptly for a day or two, you may suffer from some of the same symptoms as from too much caffeine. You may experience withdrawal headaches, for example, if you drink too much coffee during the week and much less on the weekend.

Should you or a guest get drunk, remember that caffeine is no substitute for time in counteracting the effects of alcohol. In addition, coffee gives many people a false and deadly sense of self-control.

12. Find out if you have food allergies and avoid those foods.
Most people respond stressfully to excess caffeine and sugar, but
others are allergic to even small amounts. Almost any food may
cause problems in a particular individual.

Along with caffeine and sugar, the most common problem foods
are wheat and dairy products. The symptoms, including headaches, sleepiness, irritability, and joint pain, can look like stress
and are made worse by stress.

Many people are surprised to learn that they have a powerful
craving for the very food causing the problems. Keeping a careful
food diary and rotating the suspected foods every half week may
help you and your physician discover the foods you may need to
avoid.

16

Small and Easy Ways to Eat Less and Control Your Weight

The average American gains from one half to a pound of weight annually between the ages of twenty and fifty. This middle-age spread is a strain on the heart, the back, and many other parts of the body. The causes are many, including underexercising and overeating. In addition, metabolism slows with age, so we burn fewer calories.

Being overweight is embarrassing and thus stressful to many people. The diets many choose are stressful for both the body and the mind. The guilt and failure the dieter feels when self-control is lost or weight is regained can also be stressful.

How can you reduce both the weight and the stress?

Small Changes

Middle-age spread divides up to about fifteen excess calories each day. If we could all increase our output of calories through exercise or decrease our input through dietary change, the problem would be solved.

Most people can benefit from making small changes that they can imagine doing the rest of their lives. These small changes tend to be healthy ones; they are the only ones we recommend for most people.

For the Rest of Your Life

What do we mean by small changes that you could imagine doing the rest of your life? Most of us cannot imagine eating grape-fruits or eggs or any other single food for more than a few weeks. These diets tend to be shortlived and unhealthy.

There are many smaller healthy changes that can have a powerful cumulative effect. Here is a list of ones that have been successful alone or in combination for our patients. Read through them and find one or more you could live with.

1. **Eat food only at meal times.** If you can't imagine doing this the rest of your life but weight does seem to "snack up" on you, consider the next approach.

2. **Between meals, eat only foods that can be washed.** Fresh fruits and vegetables are tasty and low in calories. The patient who discovered this small change had rejected the previous idea but found this modification helped her give up problem snacks. "After all," she said, "Twinkies taste terrible under water!"

3. **Eat food only when the television is off.** This strategy cuts down on snacking, especially after dinner. It also helps people enjoy what they are eating more fully. Of course, given the amount of television watched today, if everyone took up this habit, anorexia nervosa might replace obesity as a major public health problem.

4. **Drink a glass of water before every meal.** Many people over-eat when they are thirsty. By drinking before you eat, you avoid eating to quench your thirst. People also report they feel full sooner.

5. **Start lunch or dinner with soup or salad.** One study showed that patients who ate soup consumed an average of fifty calories less than those who did not eat soup during the meal. Starting

with soup or a green salad slows your eating and gives your body time to signal your brain that your stomach is filling up.

6. Eat only at the table. If you munch everywhere, going to the table will probably cut down on your intake because it will make eating more time-consuming and less automatic.

7. While preparing food, eat only the salad fixings. If you handle a lot of food, sticking to the salad can make a big difference.

8. Leave the serving plate on the counter, not on the table. Keeping the serving platter in the kitchen discourages nibbling: Out of sight is out of mouth. The extra steps also make overeating more of an effort.

You may also want to take the extra food off the stove and put it on a kitchen counter. When food is cold, it is less appetizing. You may also decide that warming up the food again is not worth the time and effort.

9. Turn off music before you start eating. Music makes people eat faster. One research study showed that people took more bites per minute with slow or fast music than with no music at all. Slowing down your eating allows you to enjoy your food and will help you feel full before you reach for seconds.

10. Eat no cream. This suggestion comes from Victoria Principal, a star of the television show *Dallas*. If something has the word *cream* in its name, she avoids it. For example, she eats no ice cream, cream cheese, whipped cream—or even creamed spinach. You may want to find other high-calorie foods to put on your own blacklist.

11. Eat fewer fatty foods and trim fat mercilessly. Fat has more than double the calories per ounce of other foods. In addition, the way fats are digested and enter the bloodstream, you can devour large amounts before your body notifies your brain that you have eaten.

12. Eat at least three meals a day. Skipping a meal slows your metabolism. It may also lead to overeating at the next meal. The obese tend to eat fewer meals per day than those who are thin. "I only eat one meal a day," said one of our patients. "I just never finish breakfast."

13. Always leave something on your plate. Or enough room in your stomach for your favorite food. You will avoid that overstuffed feeling. In addition, the food you don't eat may be just the fifteen calorie savings you need.

14. Brush and floss your teeth after your evening meal. Research suggests that many people eat 25 percent of their calories after dinner. By brushing and flossing right away, you may find it easy to resist food.

Clean teeth feel good and the prospect of having to repeat your dental hygiene routine may be just unpleasant enough to tip the scales in your favor.

15. Get active. Many studies show that when you go on a very low-calorie diet, your body reacts as if there is a famine and protectively slows its metabolism—by as much as 20 percent, in some instances.

If food supplies are depleted, this increased energy efficiency is good for survival. However, animal studies show that if ample food becomes available and eating is resumed, weight is regained faster and lost slower in the next cycle—the rhythm method of girth control.

The best answer to this metabolism trap—and the physical stress of yo-yo dieting—is the sort of exercise described in the last chapter.

For most people, exercise actually suppresses hunger and is really an ally in weight control. The best time of day to exercise is probably the evening because metabolism normally slows down late in the day and exercise speeds it up. Evening exercise may be healthier for other reasons, as well.

A study of dieting women who exercised before breakfast, exercised before dinner, or remained sedentary not only confirmed the importance of exercise for weight loss but also suggested that those who exercise before breakfast lose *half muscle* and half fat; while those who exercise before dinner lose mainly fat.

You may ask, what about spot reducing for love handles, thunder thighs, or pot bellies? In one study, a group of men performed five thousand situps, but the thickness of their fat pads stayed the same. Such exercise may improve your tone and appearance, but to lose the fat, you have to burn more calories. Aerobic exercise is best.

16. Fulfill your other needs. Unfortunately, food is "old reliable" for many people. It's a quick fix of pleasure, so it's overused and misused.

When you begin to overeat or to snack on high-calorie foods, ask yourself what other needs you are trying to fulfill by eating.

Also, look back over the past weeks for times when you were so involved with other things that you didn't think of food.

Plan to spend more of your time meeting your other needs in absorbing ways. Pamper yourself. Avoid deprivations of any sort and find alternate sources of pleasure.

17

Going to Your Doctor for Stress Relief

If you go to your doctor for stress relief or health enhancement, you may not find what you expected. Knowing what to expect and why can help you get the best medical care.

Stress May Not Be the Cause of Your Problem

For most of this century, technical advances in modern medicine overshadowed the growing body of research demonstrating the powerful relationship between stress and disease. The challenge was to help people understand the importance of stress.

Today, we find ourselves in the surprising position of having to remind patients and even doctors that stress is not the cause of all disease.

Why Has Stress Become So Popular?

Stress provides an attractive explanation for a variety of complaints—not just because it is so common but also because it is vague and often misunderstood. People with headaches, backaches, insomnia, anxiety, and drug addiction were once seen as weak, neurotic, or even immoral. When stress is misunderstood as arising only from difficult situations, such individuals appear as "victims" of stress and thus not responsible for their problems.

Unfortunately, this reasoning has made some stress-related diseases not only acceptable but almost fashionable. One of our patients used to show off his quadruple-bypass scar like a badge of hard work and courage.

As people learn more about the relationship between stress and illness, however, the pendulum may swing the other way. People may start seeing those suffering from stress problems as being guilty because they failed to prevent or to cure their disorders. Ideally, such extremes can be avoided and replaced by more intelligent and compassionate understanding.

As medical educators, we find that some doctors are now using stress as an explanation for all too many disorders.

For years, when doctors couldn't find a specific cause for a patient's problem, they were likely to say, "It's probably just some allergy or virus," or "There is nothing wrong with you, it's all in your head."

Now, with the flood of research studies confirming the importance of stress in so many complaints and diseases, we have to remind some student physicians to keep their stethoscopes on and to do a thorough medical workup before dismissing a problem as stress.

What You Can Expect from Your Physician

Most doctors practicing today were trained to treat illness rather than to prevent it. The traditional medical curriculum provided little instruction in health maintenance or the role of emotions in producing illness.

Preventive medicine was devoted largely to the use of vaccines or to public health sanitation measures. For health enhancement, some attention may have been given to nutrition or vitamins, but very little, if any, to the value of exercise, relaxation training, or other forms of stress management.

According to Richard Palmer, a past president of the American Medical Association, "Only 10 percent of all factors that cause illness are factors that physicians are trained to treat."

Many of these problems are changing. Recently, medical schools have added divisions or departments of behavioral medicine. However, even the well-educated physician, just out of school, may disappoint the consumer. Public awareness and knowledge, sparked by media coverage of new medical information, is sometimes greater than that of the average physician. Newspapers, magazines, radio, and television regularly report the latest research from respected medical journals days before the physician receives a copy in the mail or has had the opportunity to read about and evaluate new developments.

Searching for Doctors with Skills Instead of Pills

Patients are increasingly wary of the unknown and long-term side effects of medications. For these and other reasons, more and more people are seeking nutritional and other drugfree approaches, not only to treat illness but to enhance health.

People are searching for doctors offering skills rather than pills. However, few physicians really know how to respond effectively to young or middle-age adults with no medical problems who request specific advice on maintaining or on improving their health.

Physicians themselves are often struggling unsuccessfully to modify the way they eat, drink, smoke, exercise, and relax. In fact, partly due to the stress of their occupations, physicians die four years earlier, on the average, and are more likely to have problems with alcohol, drug abuse, and even suicide than others of similar age and social status.

Why Is It So Hard to Find a Doctor with These Skills?

One of the reasons it is difficult to find a health-oriented doctor is that health insurance pays primarily for the treatment of illness. Furthermore, insurance generally rewards the physician for performing expensive tests and procedures. Reimbursable activities involve doing something to the patient rather than thinking, teaching or caring. Rapidly increasing malpractice suits further encourage and justify the emphasis on costly tests and procedures.

Patients also expect the physician to "do something." Similarly, they not only expect but are most willing to pay for tests, injections, or surgery. Patients are reluctant to pay for expertise and time spent in providing insight, instruction, or behavioral modification that could prevent future problems. In fact, for every $100 we spend on health care in this country, less than $5 goes for illness prevention.

Given the present financial reward system and high malpractice premiums, it takes a very dedicated and special doctor to devote precious office time and risk losing income to learn and to apply behavioral and preventive medicine techniques. In the next chapter, we will provide some suggestions to help you find the best physician for you.

18

Avoiding the New Snake-Oil by Forming a Partnership with Your Doctor

The changes described in the previous chapter have created a void in medical care, which has been rapidly filled by a variety of alternative providers and programs. Not surprisingly, it has also attracted large numbers of entrepreneurs, zealots, and even charlatans. As a result, it is often quite difficult for patients and even health professionals to evaluate the legitimacy of such activities and services.

How can you sift through the conflicting claims inside and outside the conventional medical system? How can you judge the pros and cons, advantages and disadvantages of so many different approaches to your health?

What Is a Patient to Do?

There are no clear answers, only many questions. Our advice, however, would be to find and to retain a sympathetic, caring physician, sensitive to your concerns and willing to direct you to the best resources to satisfy your needs.

If you are looking for such assistance, you might want to obtain a list of local physicians who are members of reputable national organizations devoted to preventive medicine or holistic health approaches (see chapter 37). Many physicians are active members of health clubs or fitness centers. Contacting such facilities for referrals or suggestions may be helpful. Local, county, and state medical societies, as well as medical schools, may be able to identify other doctors with specific interests, skills, and training in areas of nutrition, exercise, or stress reduction.

A Shared Responsibility

Other important questions are just how much responsibility for your health you should assume and at what point it is appropriate to seek professional advice or guidance.

The answers depend on a variety of factors that would include your medical condition, the risk-to-benefit ratio of taking total responsibility, the breadth and depth of your knowledge in the areas of concern, and the experience and attitude of your physician.

The doctor–patient relationship should ideally be a partnership based on mutual respect, confidence, and understanding. It is a rare or insensitive physician who fails to learn something from patients. On the other hand, the "educated consumer" is not always the "best customer" because misinformation abounds. Many approaches to health offer more hype than help.

A concerned and compassionate physician is still your best guide and partner through these troubled waters.

How the Partnership Approaches Medication and Stress Relief

Treating hypertension is a good example. Over 60 million Americans suffer from this disorder. While there is considerable controversy about exercise, diet (salt, calcium, potassium, magnesium, fats, etc.), and stress reduction in the treatment of hypertension, the National Heart, Lung, and Blood Institute's guidelines urge such nondrug approaches as the first step for most patients. Many individuals take up such activities with enthusiasm.

In many instances, such measures are used in combination with conventional blood pressure medications. This combination may result in lowering drug requirements or making current dosage schedules more potent or even toxic.

Given the risks associated with the treatment of hypertension and heart disease, it might be really hazardous for any patient to decide arbitrarily to change a therapeutic program without a physician's guidance.

Antianxiety Drugs

Many medications used to treat high blood pressure or angina are also prescribed to relieve other stress-related complaints, such as headache. Inderal and other beta blockers, for example, while officially approved primarily for cardiovascular problems, are frequently used to prevent stage fright, examination jitters, and stress-related tremors.

Your physician may prescribe an antianxiety drug or tranquilizer for your stress-related symptoms. Don't immediately assume you need to find a new doctor. Such prescriptions are usually safe, appropriate, and effective for relieving acute or short-term stress while you are learning other and more permanent ways to deal with your problems.

Tranquilizers and sedatives can be valuable aids in managing a variety of stress-related complaints. Unfortunately, because of adverse publicity, it is often very difficult to convince some patients to take such drugs when they really could be beneficial.

If you have been on tranquilizers for more than a year, however, you might want to ask your physician to reassess your needs and your therapeutic program. One of the authors found that one out of every four long-term tranquilizer users enrolling in a withdrawal program was depressed rather than anxious. Once depression is identified, more appropriate and effective medication and therapy can provide greater benefits.

Biofeedback May Reduce Drug Requirements

Research has shown that, in addition to high blood pressure and anxiety, there are a number of diseases and disorders for which relaxation or biofeedback have proved capable of eliminating or sharply reducing the need for drug treatment. Diabetes, headaches, backaches, insomnia, panic disorder, angina, and depression are examples of such conditions.

If you are taking medications for any of these disorders, you may feel greater effects from your drugs as you become more experienced with stress-relief techniques. Consequently, dosages may constantly need to be adjusted and lowered. The best judge of that, however, should be your concerned and caring physician-partner who is knowledgeable about the indications, advantages, and limitations of all such approaches as they apply specifically to you.

Ten Prescriptions for Handling Your Body's Stress

1. Breathe slowly and deeply from your stomach area.
2. Relax your muscles with tension-and-release cycles or recall relaxation.
3. Imagine that you are an old rag doll—loose, limp, and relaxed.
4. Give yourself a six-second tranquilizer before answering the phone and while you wait in traffic, during commercials, and in cashiers' lines.
5. Use your *pocket guide* for biofeedback to raise your hand temperature above 90 degrees.
6. Avoid stress-inducing foods and seasonings.
7. Do not smoke or chew tobacco.
8. Control your weight by making small permanent changes in what, when, and how you eat.
9. Use one of nature's best tranquilizers—exercise regularly.
10. Form a partnership with a competent, concerned, and caring physician.

Relieving
the
Stress
of Your
Mind

19

What Makes Most People Miserable?

A Billion-Dollar Misery Contest

Imagine a contest in which a billion dollars would be awarded to the person who could achieve the greatest emotional misery for thirty days. Misery is to be judged by imaginary "emotionometers" that measure the depth of all emotions.

What would you do if you wanted to win the contest? Physical torture and poisons might be painful, but knowing you could be revived and win might keep you from feeling sufficiently miserable. Great losses of all kinds might be endured with only mild levels of misery, because you would know what the money could bring you later.

How could you make yourself depressed, angry, lonely, or guilt-ridden enough to register extreme misery on the emotionometers? Unfortunately, many people are doing a very good job at this already. However, if asked, they would probably be unable to explain their "secret" or how they could use it to relieve their misery.

How to Make Yourself Miserable

The royal road to misery is described by the words of the ancient philosopher Epictetus: "Men are disturbed not by things, but by the view which they take of them." To win the contest, you would have to change radically the way you see and think about things.

For example, to become depressed, you might force yourself to think that everything is hopeless; to become angry, that everything is unfair; to become lonely, that everyone has deserted you; to feel guilt-ridden, that you have done the unforgivable; and to become stressed, that everything is dangerous.

It might require a constant struggle to convince yourself, "I never do anything right, I'm going through all this for nothing," or, "Even if I win, nobody will love me; they'll only love my money and I'll probably get robbed and fall for lots of bad investments."

Some torture and misfortune might help, but ultimately, the thoughts of the participants would decide the winner.

What You Think Is What You Feel

Ideally, this exercise has helped you better appreciate the powerful relationship between thinking and feeling. Understanding this relationship is one of the most important keys to relieving the stress of your mind. If what you think is what you feel, the best way to change your stressful feelings is to change your stressful thoughts.

How can you change these thoughts? The next chapter will help you recognize your most stressful thoughts quickly. The other chapters in this section will help you to stop them and replace them with healthier thoughts and images.

20

Recognizing Stressful Thoughts

Anger and anxiety are the emotional equivalents of the body's fight-or-flight response. These emotions are useful signals that something may be wrong and may need attention.

Unfortunately, if we overreact with anger and anxiety, we can trip ourselves up and send our bodies into overdrive. These exaggerated responses can also interfere with doing the very things that need to be done.

One way to find the stressful thoughts behind our emotional overreactions is to start with the feelings and work backward to find the thoughts.

Finding the Fire behind the Smoke

Think of your stressful emotions as smoke and your thoughts as fire. Smoke is not only unpleasant, but it can keep us from seeing what started the fire and what we need to do about it. In addition, the smoke is often far worse than the fire.

When you feel upset, imagine that the emotion is setting off a smoke alarm in your mind. Look for the fire by instantly asking yourself, "What am I thinking?"

Exaggerated Thoughts Are Stressful Thoughts

What kind of thoughts are stressful? Most stressful thoughts are exaggerated thoughts. For example, many people think that they *must* do something. What they really mean is that it would be *better* if they did something.

Must makes it sound as if erring or delaying something would be dangerous. *Musterbation* can lead to hurry-up sickness and persecutory perfectionism. Other stressful words to watch out for include *should, ought, have to, owe,* and *deserve.*

Many of the labels people use to refer to themselves and others are also exaggerated and stressful thoughts. When people say they are *crazy, lazy, stupid, sinful, ugly, weak,* or *clumsy,* the idea of being 100 percent any of these qualities is upsetting. Some days we may be 85 percent stupid, but saying we are *stupid* fails to recognize the remaining 15 percent—which can make us feel worthless or frighteningly defective.

There are many unhealthy and stressful thoughts. Have you ever said to yourself, "I have to be perfect," or "Everyone has to like me," or "I have to help everyone," or "I'll never succeed because of my past"?

Beware of any exaggerations. Exaggerated thoughts bring on exaggerated emotions.

When Are You Going to . . . ?

How many times have you been asked when you were going to grow up or to wise up and do something? People want to know when you plan to get married, when you plan to have children, and when you are going to get a job.

These questions may be well meaning, but they often arise out of the anxieties of the asker. Such questions can be annoying. They can also plant the seeds of self-doubt.

Once you have made a well-considered decision, watch out for the thoughts such questions can evoke. After all, before you know it, people will be asking when you're going to retire and when you're going to die!

Sometimes it is best not to answer a question or to question the basis for the inquiry. You do not have to explain your actions. You may decide to say, "I have my reasons." If asked what those reasons might be, you can say, "I don't feel the need to justify my decisions."

The Shadow of a Saber-Toothed Tiger

In the beginning of this book, we asked you to imagine that you were a cave dweller confronted by the shadow of a saber-toothed tiger. We detailed many of your body's fight-or-flight responses and discussed their survival value should you be faced with a battle for your life. However, if what you saw had been the shadow of a tree leaning over in the moonlight—and not the shadow of a saber-toothed tiger—your responses would have had very little survival value.

Knowledge Is Power . . .

For many people, stress is triggered by shadows, because they fail to get enough information.

One of our patients, a young teacher named Mary, complained of stomach distress. She reported that her principal had been supportive and enthusiastic about her teaching at the beginning of the year, but now he was distant and hardly talked to her.

Mary wasn't enjoying her work anymore and thought the principal might not recommend that the board renew her contract. She also worried about having turned down his request that she lead another after-school activity.

When Mary returned for her next visit, she was beaming. Asked why, she reported, "My principal—his mother died and he's in debt. Isn't it great?" Then, she laughed, a little embarrassed at what she had said.

If you jump to conclusions, see the cup half empty, or take things personally, you are casting some long shadows. It's time to put a flashlight to your situations and thoughts. Remove the shadows and relieve your stress.

. . . But Ignorance Is Bliss

What if you seem to focus on all the irritating things others do? Start ignoring the petty faults, particularly once you have asked for change. If you can't, ask yourself what the bigger problem might be and what you might do about it.

Begin appreciating your strengths rather than focusing on your deficits. Keep the little annoyances of life in perspective. When things break down, remember that they can be fixed or replaced. As one patient said, "I'm starting to ignore the weeds and now I can enjoy the flowers."

Still More Shadows

Watch out for other stressful shadows, too; for some, their shadows are those of a past they regret or of a future they fear. Beware of your stressful thoughts of yesterday and tomorrow—they can rob you of today.

21

Stop, Look, and Listen

Stop

If you catch yourself listening to negative thoughts, daydreaming nightmares, or feeling overwhelmed, mentally yell, "Stop!" If the thoughts reappear, repeat your mental command. Several *Stops!* will usually derail your unhealthy thoughts, images, and feelings.

This simple but powerful procedure is a well-researched stress-management technique known in the professional literature as thought-stopping.

For many minor negative thoughts or bad feelings, thought-stopping alone will be sufficient to halt the stress response at the level of your mind. If *Stop* is not enough, you can add *Look* and *Listen* to the recipe.

Look

Immediately after you say *Stop!* use your mind's eye to imagine a large, red stop sign. See the letters STOP and put the brakes on your thoughts.

Another image people use is a red traffic light. Some find a flashing red light to be a more effective signal.

Still another visual image is a large, imposing police officer with his hand up, signaling *Stop*. Be sure to see the blue uniform and bright, shiny badge.

Listen

Another mental breaker is the use of a sound in addition to images and the word *Stop*. For example, you might use the police image and have the officer "blow the whistle" on your thought. Another combination might be to hear the horn of a train and see yourself stopping at the crossing.

Repetitive, exaggerated thoughts are stressful. They warrant the strongest images to stop their threat to your health and productivity.

A few people find that mentally yelling *Stop!* or seeing a police officer triggers stress. If you do, try using a large, imaginary eraser to wipe clean the blackboard of your mind. Or deposit your thoughts into an imaginary metal box, shut the heavy lid, attach a big padlock, and throw away the key.

Use whatever technique you find most effective and as often as needed, until the thoughts are extinguished. For some patients, this may be thirty to forty times a day.

Once you have recognized your stressful thoughts and stopped them, you can substitute healthier, more productive thoughts with positive self-talk.

22

Food for Thought

In the last two chapters you learned how to recognize stressful thinking and how to stop it. Now you are ready to replace it with stress-resistant and health-enhancing thoughts.

Where can you find such thoughts, how can you develop them, and what can you do to maximize their use in your life?

One of the best ways to answer these questions is to have you look at thoughts as food for the mind. If exaggerated and stressful thoughts are like junk food, productive and pleasurable thoughts are like health food. We need to be as careful with what we put into our brains as we are with what we put into our bodies.

Science has identified a number of basic food groups; supermarkets offer a wide variety of healthy foods, and you can even grow some yourself. Ultimately, the choice is yours. And so it is with what you feed your mind. Let's start with some basic food groups for your mind.

The Three Cs of the Stress-Resistant Personality

Psychologists studying telephone company executives during the divestiture of AT&T confirmed that rapid change can lead to disease, but they also predicted with great accuracy which executives would best resist the ill effects of stress. The most powerful predictions were made by measuring what can be called the three Cs of the stress-resistant personality.

The hundred executives who scored high on feelings of *commitment*, *control*, and *challenge* when faced with change suffered only half as much illness as the hundred who scored low on those factors. Those executives who succumbed to stress felt alienated rather than committed, powerless rather than in control, and threatened rather than challenged by new situations.

A number of our workshop participants have found this information easy to apply by remembering the three Cs when they face stressful situations. However, there are also more specific ways of developing these qualities. One of the best is to cultivate and to use the thoughts that support each of these healthy approaches to stress.

Commitment

You might want to spend some time pinpointing the relationships and goals that are most meaningful in your life. For example, if you have a job, write down what you contribute to society. As jobs become more automated and work more subdivided, we need to remember the basic human needs each of our jobs fulfill.

Wedding anniversaries and family reunions help us to reaffirm other commitments. Find a couple of words to summarize your commitments or photographs to portray them. By doing so, you will be able to draw instantly on the words or pictures to evoke feelings of commitment when you feel alienated.

If you find yourself wanting to do things that you can't do because of other things you *have to* do, you may feel burdened rather than committed. In reality, we don't *have to* do anything—we choose to do almost everything we do. Yes, there are consequences for failing to do the *have to*s, but thinking about those consequences will either clarify our commitments or help us make new, more meaningful ones.

If you know where you are going, brief thoughts about your commitments will help you to rise above day-to-day setbacks.

Religious Commitment

It is not for us as doctors to do more than state the importance of meeting your spiritual needs. Religious faith can be the greatest source of strength and commitment. Pastoral counseling can also be of immense value in the relief of stress.

Consider just some of the measurable benefits of religion for each of the three sources of stress. A relaxed body is one of the side effects of quiet prayer. Religious fellowship is an important source of social support during situational stress. Brief prayers can help you quickly find a religious perspective to relieve the stress of your mind.

Control

One way of increasing your sense of control is to remember the saying: *You can't smooth out the surf, but you can learn to ride the waves.* In other words, we may not be able to control the world, but we can control our responses to the world. The techniques in this book are designed to help you gain greater control of your responses to the ups and downs of life.

Identifying areas in your life where you do have control can also prevent feelings of powerlessness. If your job or your home life seems temporarily out of control, you may want to find or devote more time to a hobby or to a part-time job.

When you feel powerless, put a stop to the thoughts behind the feeling and think about these other activities. Doing this will instantly bring you a greater sense of control.

Worrying Can Be Controlled

Let's say you find yourself thinking about your problems and feeling out of control. Ask yourself, "Am I worrying, or am I planning?"

If you are planning, then make sure you have sufficient time, information, and tools to develop, assess, and write down your plans. If not, schedule time to plan.

If you are worrying, either use thought-stopping and then do something worthwhile, or put aside a particular half-hour each day and postpone your worrying until then. Studies show worrying for ten to twenty minutes tends to increase fears, but one long worry session decreases the time wasted each day by an average of 35 percent.

To regain control when you feel you *have to* do things, actually substitute the words *I'm choosing to* for *I have to*. This shift will remind you that you are the master, not the slave, of your life.

If you have allowed yourself to become a victim of other people's demands, learning the skills in the section on situational stress will also help you set yourself free.

Your sense of control also depends on your expectations. If you expect to feed, bathe, and put three young children to bed in an hour, you will probably feel as out of control as a father we know felt the first night his wife went out of town. Don't set yourself up for frustration with unrealistic expectations.

Business and professional goals also need to be challenging, but not out of reach. Once you succeed, beware of inflating your self-expectations and setting yourself up for stress and disappointment.

Challenge

One of the things we are guaranteed in life, along with death and taxes, is change. If you see change as threatening and overwhelming, you only increase your stress. If you see change as full of hidden possibilities, your life can become an adventure rather than a burden.

How do you see the problems you face? Regularly substituting the word *challenge* for *problem* will help to remind you of the opportunity and adventure that lie in store.

A "Wonderful" Challenge

When someone brings you what at first sounds like bad news, stop and look for the seeds of exciting solutions. A businessman we know likes to surprise people around him when he hears of a problem by immediately exclaiming, "Wonderful!" Then, he is challenged to find a way to attack the problem creatively.

In *Future Shock*, Alvin Toffler vividly described how the rate of change is accelerating faster today than any time in our history. In many areas of life, it may be best to go beyond improving our response to change.

The businessman we just described wanted us to point out that, in the future, those who adapt quickly to changes will barely keep up. The real winners will *create* the changes.

Most of us, but especially those suffering from rustout, should accept the challenge of the future and become change creators.

23

Health-Food Stores of the Mind

The news media offers a daily dose of woes, but there are also writers and speakers who specialize in positive thinking. We need to know what is wrong with our world, but we also need the resources to solve its problems creatively.

Finding a Health-Food Store for Positive Thinking

Where can you look for pleasurable and productive thoughts and how can you keep them available for easy access?

Books are obvious sources, and we have compiled a short list for your consideration in appendix II. Every book on the list meets two requirements: It clearly helped one or more of our patients, and it is compatible with the literature in our fields of psychology and medicine.

You may want to start a file of stress-relieving quotations and memorize the most helpful ones. Sources are everywhere, but when you hear or read one that resonates with your needs, write it down immediately.

One of the authors and his wife, a child psychologist, found just such a quote when they needed relief from the stress caused by their crying, colicky baby. After they had tried almost everything anyone had ever told them to try, they would take turns rocking their baby and think, "This too will pass."

Here are some of our favorite sayings for stress management. Many are gifts from patients. Some of the anonymous quotations may have known authors. If this is the case, we ask to be forgiven.

"If only I may grow firmer, simpler, quieter, warmer."
—*Dag Hammarskjold*

Two rules for stress management: "Rule one: Don't sweat the small stuff. Rule two: It's all small stuff."
—*Robert Eliot*

"He who is content with little has everything."
—*Anonymous*

"Happiness is not having what you want—it's wanting what you have."
—*Spencer Johnson*

"Some of the best things in life are missed because they cost nothing."
—*Anonymous*

"The secret of life is enjoying the passage of time."
—*James Taylor*

"Life is not having and getting but being and becoming."
—*Anonymous*

"Ask yourself, 'Will it really matter five years from now?'"
—*Anonymous*

"The true worth of a man is to be measured by the objects he pursues."
—*Anonymous*

"You cannot be anything if you want to be everything."
—*Anonymous*

"Take me the way I am—if you like me, great; if not, so be it."
—*A patient who used the phrase to stop feeling "like a pretzel"*

"Life is full of miserableness, loneliness, unhappiness; and it's over too quickly."

—*Woody Allen*

"To live is to suffer, to survive is to find meaning in the suffering."

—*Victor Frankl, M.D.*

"We arrive in this world alone. We depart alone. This time called life was meant to share."

—*Anonymous*

"If we are afraid to be wrong, we may never know what it is to be right."

—*Elliott Gould*

"Our doubts are traitors and make us lose the good we oft might win by fearing to attempt."

—*William Shakespeare*

"If you never want to make a mistake, do nothing, say nothing, be nothing."

—*Anonymous*

"Whether you think you can or you can't, you're probably right."

—*Henry Ford*

"Anything worth doing, is worth doing poorly—the first time."

—*Anonymous*

"All things are difficult before they are easy."

—*John Norlay*

"No one was ever born goof-proof."

—*Anonymous*

"Moderation in all things but prayer."

—*Anonymous*

"If any man seeks for greatness, let him forget greatness and ask for truth and he will find both."

—*Thomas Mann*

"If you compare yourself with others, you may become vain and bitter: for always there will be greater and lesser persons than yourself."

—*"Desiderata"*

"The important thing is this: to be able at any moment to sacrifice what we are for what we could become."

—*Charles Du Bois*

"If you do the thing you fear, the fear will disappear."

—*Anonymous*

"When you are talking to yourself, watch your language."

—*Dennis Waitley*

"Happiness is an inside job."

—*bumper sticker*

"I am an old man and have known a great many troubles—but most of them never happened."

—*Mark Twain*

"I've just decided to dread one day at a time."

—*Isaac Asimov*

"Can anybody remember when times were not hard and money was not scarce?"

—*Ralph Waldo Emerson*

"Taking one step at a time is best in the long run."

—*Chinese fortune cookie*

"Ask yourself, 'Is it worth dying for?'"

—*Robert Eliot and Dennis Breo*

"To live continually in thoughts of ill will, cynicism, suspicion, and envy is to be confined in a self-made prison cell."

—*James Allen*

"In an insane society, a sane person must appear insane."

—*Star Trek*

"It isn't the burdens of today that drive men mad. Rather, it is regret over yesterday or fear of tomorrow. Regret and fear are twin thieves who would rob us of today."

—*Robert J. Hastings*

"People are about as happy as they make up their minds to be."

—*Abraham Lincoln*

"Nothing can bring you peace but yourself."
—*Ralph Waldo Emerson*

"Man's mind, once stretched by a new idea, never regains its original dimensions."

—*Oliver Wendell Holmes*

"With knowledge comes opportunity. With perseverance comes success."

—*J. C. Johnstone*

"Men do not fail—they give up trying."
—*Anonymous*

If you suffer from heart disease and you are hostile or time-urgent, one of the most successful therapy approaches is described in *Treating Type A Behavior and Your Heart* by Meyer Friedman, M.D., and Diane Ulmer, R.N., M.S. In the back of the book are sixty-three phrases they used in their program. Here are four anyone might want to consider:

"For every minute you are angry, you lose sixty seconds of happiness."

—*Ralph Waldo Emerson*

"Before I had my heart attack, I didn't have any friends. When I played poker, I played to win from the bastards."

—*Jesse Lair*

"Ask yourself why you are so much more aware of the irritating qualities of other persons than their good qualities."

—*Anonymous*

"You shall have joy or you shall have power, said God, you shall not have both."

—*Ralph Waldo Emerson*

Giving Yourself Permission to Slow Down and Enjoy Life

Even if you are free of hostility, you may be suffering from the stress of rushing through life and you may not be fully enjoying life. You have hurry-up sickness. There are many approaches to this problem. One is to memorize healthy thoughts and give yourself permission to enjoy life. Here are a few powerful ones:

"There is more to life than increasing its speed."

—*Kenneth Grooms*

"Life is not a destiny, but a journey to be enjoyed."

—*Anonymous.*

"Live each day as if it was your last because someday you're going to be right."

—*Anonymous*

"He who is hurried cannot walk gracefully."

—*Chinese proverb*

Healthy thoughts are also available on audiocassettes. Portable tape players and automobile cassette decks make it possible to learn and to memorize healthy thoughts while you do other things.

We have listed some of the best audio programs in appendix II. If a program is not widely available in bookstores, we have included an address for mail order. The tapes listed meet the same requirements we used for books.

Short Is Powerful

Look for brief thoughts or shorten some of the thoughts you find. To avoid programming "someday" beliefs about life in general, use the present tense and a first-person pronoun. Change "If you try to please everyone, you will please no one, including yourself," for example, to "I don't have to please anyone except myself."

It may also be helpful to stretch yourself in new directions with bold messages like, "I work more creatively under pressure," or "It's easy for me to be self-confident."

142

Making the Most of the Thoughts You Collect

Once you have found some good food for thought, you may want to repeat and memorize the ideas when you are deeply relaxed. By freeing yourself of tension and distraction, you learn more effectively and you are more likely to remember the thoughts when you need instant stress relief.

If you repeat healthy thoughts hundreds of times while relaxed and stressed, these thoughts will gradually become the first to surface in difficult situations and there will be far less stress to relieve.

To build confidence, take the time to soak in your success. Many of us today are so busy pursuing the next goal that we are blind to our accomplishments and never nurture our sense of competency. As with other healthy ideas, it is best to focus on your achievements when you are fully relaxed.

Building Self-Confidence

Susan, one of our workshop participants, enthusiastically accepted a better-paying managerial position at a new firm. Things went well for a few days until she had to take some disciplinary actions. Susan complained she lacked confidence. She desperately wanted to make a good first impression.

Susan had been growing professionally at a very rapid pace. We recommended that she change her self-image through a relaxed review of her skills and accomplishments. Susan spent a few evenings building a reservoir of healthy beliefs. At work, she tapped into this reservoir by thinking, "I have succeeded before, and in time, I'll prove myself here, too."

Becoming a Live Disk Jockey

When you learned right from wrong, your parents also taught you many things about yourself. Unfortunately, when you did not listen, they may have added a lot of "negative nonsense."

Some of us are now handicapped with such thoughts as: "Johnny, you are so stupid," "Nancy, you are impossible to live with," and "I don't think you will ever be able to do anything right." These old thoughts will be the first to surface unless we soak in new thoughts. Once you learn healthier thoughts, you also need to put them to use.

Dr. Dennis Knave, one of our psychiatry residents, explained it this way. When your feelings are stressful, they are usually the result of old tapes. Some are from our childhoods; others are from more recent disappointments. As the disk jockeys of our minds, we sometimes get lazy and just play the old, canned tapes. These are boring and out-of-date. The goal is to broadcast "live" more of the time and to choose the music you really want to hear.

Stress-Free Self-Talk

Thought can also be understood as what we tell ourselves about our world. Many psychologists call thought "self-talk." If you call thought "self-talk," you acknowledge that it does not descend on you or possess you, but rather that you create it.

So, if your mind is full of negative self-chatter, wake up and get to work. Take the stress out of what you tell yourself and replace it with more productive and pleasurable self-talk.

24

Those Who Laugh, Last

One of the healthiest things to substitute for a stressful thought is a humorous one. As Art Linkletter says, "Humor is life's greatest lubricant." You might agree, but how can you develop a sense of humor?

The Psychology of Humor

The psychology of humor is complex, but we know that the unexpected plays a major role in what makes people laugh. Interestingly enough, although exaggerated thoughts can be stressful, unexpected or even further exaggerated thoughts can be very humorous. A host of comedians have laughed with us all the way to the bank by poking fun at themselves with routines that exaggerate their faults and troubles.

We may not want to become comedians, but by exaggerating an exaggerated thought, we can learn to laugh at the world and get a perspective on our problems. Humor also reminds us that most of our problems are not unique and that we are not alone.

As Dr. Peter Hanson points out in his book *The Joy of Stress*, to maximize the benefits of humor, learn to exaggerate your faults and to laugh at yourself. Remember, "If you cannot laugh at yourself, you will find plenty of volunteers to do it for you!"

Start studying cartoons and jokes to find out what makes them funny. Take time to see the situation comedies around you instead of waiting to watch them on prime time.

Humor springs from the mind and can relieve its stress, but humor can also be used to manage the other two sources of distress—laughter can release stress from the body as well as lighten stressful situations.

Internal Jogging

Laughter is great for the body. Some have called it "internal jogging" because it increases your heart rate, breathing activity, blood pressure, body temperature, and natural pain-killing chemicals. Muscles tense as we wait for the punch line, contract as we laugh, and relax profoundly—for up to forty-five minutes—as we recover from the excitement of laughing. Heart rate and blood pressure then drop below prelaugh levels.

One study found that laughter reduced stress about as much as biofeedback training. Is laughter the best medicine? Its curative powers and relationship to longevity are just now being explored.

Situational Humor

Those who laugh not only last but succeed. Humor can be a powerful tool in tense situations, and its cumulative effect on a daily basis may be of even greater importance. As one executive said, "We get a lot done and enjoy doing it here because we take our work seriously, but we don't take ourselves seriously." No wonder his business was so successful.

An operating nurse we treated combined imagery and humor to calm her fear of an overbearing surgeon. Each time the surgeon raised his voice and shoulders in anger, she would imagine his toupee rotating like a helicopter. This image relieved both her mind

and her situational stress because she no longer got flustered or
made as many mistakes.

Laughing with Others

According to one report, Americans laugh an average of fifteen
times a day. Do you? To get your fair share, you might consider
spending more time with people who make you laugh.

If you want to use more humor, introduce it slowly but regularly.
Start at home and in social situations where there is little of importance to be lost. Use a brief relaxation technique and take the
plunge. Gradually, you'll enjoy taking a playful attitude toward
more and more things in life.

As with all stress strategies, humor must be used in moderation.
However, in proper doses, its benefits are many.

25

Using Your Imagination for Relaxing and Rehearsing

For years, people have been counting sheep to fall asleep. The practice succeeds because it takes advantage of what is now known about the two sides of the brain.

By counting, you bore the logical and verbal left side of your brain. By watching fluffy sheep jump over a fence, you bore the visual–spatial right side of your brain. When both sides of the brain are bored, stress is relieved and sleep can occur.

In the last few chapters, you learned how to use healthy thinking to replace rapidly the stressful thoughts of your left brain. The verbal humor of the last chapter can be considered a bridge to the more creative right brain. This chapter will help you use the healthy imagery of your right brain to relieve stress.

Vacationing in Your Mind

To learn visual imagery, you will need a few minutes in a quiet place where you will not be disturbed. Set the stage with any combination of other relaxation techniques. Then, find a scene that is personally relaxing for you.

The scene may be a beautiful place that anyone would find

profoundly relaxing or it may be a place with special meaning for you. Perhaps you visited or lived there at a time in your life when you felt most at peace with the world.

The key to imagery is combining all your senses. Enrich what you see with sounds, textures, tastes, and smells. Make your images come alive. The scenes below will help you understand what we mean and develop your skill of imaging.

If you cannot think of a personally relaxing place, you may want to create a scene where you can imagine yourself totally and completely relaxed. Here are a few to consider.

Sightseeing for Relaxation

See yourself on a comfortable summer day, lying on a sandy beach below a clear blue sky. The glow of the sun bathes your body in warmth. The sand molds to your body, supporting every muscle. The cries of the sea gulls accent the waves lapping the shore. You can taste the salt air.

Now, visualize yourself lying in a hammock on a perfect fall day with a light breeze rustling the multicolored leaves. See the azure blue sky and cotton-white clouds overhead. Perhaps you are next to a shimmering lake.

For still more practice, imagine sailing in a light breeze or watching a fiery sunset. Try sitting in a mountain cabin with a crackling fire, sipping a favorite drink. Whatever you choose to fantasize is fine, as long as it is profoundly relaxing.

You can use imagery for long and short periods of time, depending on the desired effects. If you want to relax deeply for twenty minutes, you may want to add your favorite instrumental music or an environmental recording.

These relaxation retreats can be used instead of coffee breaks for renewed energy. However, after you have practiced this a few times, you may want to start using your imagery for immediate stress relief.

Take an Instant Vacation

The best images for instant stress relief are very brief and pre-planned. Find a key word to remind you of your most relaxing scene. One of our patients used the word *Pensacola* because of her favorite vacation spot in Florida. Others use the names of their favorite mountains, beaches, and rivers.

You can use your key word anytime and anywhere to help you clear your mind of distressing thoughts and take a relaxing mental vacation. Instant vacations can also be used to relieve the stress of boredom. Recently, a workshop participant described it this way, "The greatest magic carpet is your imagination."

Flying to Tahiti during Board Meetings

One of our patients is a lawyer who sits on the board of a large corporation. Having recovered from burnout, he enjoys telling people how he now uses visual imagery to vacation in Tahiti during long meetings.

When people are concerned that it might prove embarrassing, he explains that no one on the board suspects because he has recultivated the interested look of a law student. If asked his opinion about a proposal, he pauses and answers thoughtfully, "Perhaps." If this is the wrong answer, he says the other board members look at him strangely and he answers calmly, "Well, maybe not."

We do not recommend using visual imagery to the neglect of other duties, but we were pleased to hear that his sense of humor had returned.

Using Imagery to Go Beyond Relaxation

Different pictures unlock different emotions. If you want to relax, you can use the most relaxing of the scenes you have practiced. If you feel defeated, you may want to use the image of your proudest moment to restore your self-confidence. If you are tired but want to continue an important activity, you might use a vivid picture of the final goal you are pursuing. If you are distracted by loneliness, you may want to use the image of a time when you were close to a loved one.

Review your life for images of special people, places, and times you might use. These make up your psychological security box. If you know the contents, you can get what you need on emotionally stormy days.

150

Again, it is best to have key words for these pictures. For example, many people use *graduation* as a key word to remember their feelings of pride, relief, and joy when they graduated from high school, college, or professional school.

Putting the Key Words Where You Can Find Them

When you have found a key word for one of these special moments, you may want to write it down on your *pocket guide* in the space shown in figure 11. If you find more than one and run out of room there, turn over the *pocket guide* and use the space around your name and address.

Finding a Wise Man or Woman through Imagery

When you have an important decision to make and want to be sure you are exploring all your options, it is helpful to seek advice from family and friends. However, when the important people in your life are not available, you might imagine having lunch with them and asking for their advice. Imagine what each might suggest. Another approach is to imagine what each person might do if they faced the same situation.

Additional ideas may come from imagining a meeting with a wise old man or woman who sits with you in a quiet place and counsels you. This experience is often very productive and reassuring.

Additional Uses of Instant Imagery

It is said that imagination is the key to motivation. If you want to motivate yourself or others, you can replace failing willpower and idle threat-power with creative pull-power.

What You See Is What You Get

If you are facing a challenging activity that makes you anxious, you may want to do some image rehearsal. Rather than worry about the activity, use your mind to improve your performance.

For major undertakings, you might practice weeks in advance.

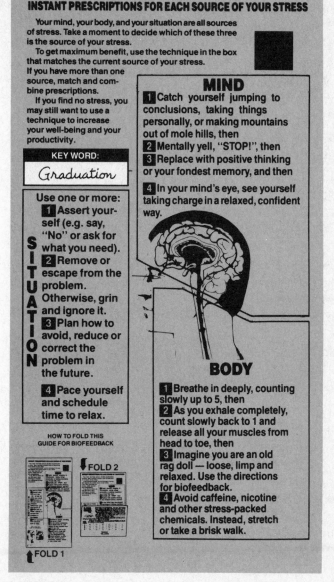

INSTANT PRESCRIPTIONS FOR EACH SOURCE OF YOUR STRESS

Your mind, your body, and your situation are all sources of stress. Take a moment to decide which of these three is the source of your stress.

To get maximum benefit, use the technique in the box that matches the current source of your stress.

If you have more than one source, match and combine prescriptions.

If you find no stress, you may still want to use a technique to increase your well-being and your productivity.

KEY WORD:

Graduation

Use one or more:
1 Assert yourself (e.g. say, "No" or ask for what you need).
2 Remove or escape from the problem. Otherwise, grin and ignore it.
3 Plan how to avoid, reduce or correct the problem in the future.
4 Pace yourself and schedule time to relax.

SITUATION

HOW TO FOLD THIS GUIDE FOR BIOFEEDBACK

↓FOLD 2

↑FOLD 1

MIND
1 Catch yourself jumping to conclusions, taking things personally, or making mountains out of mole hills, then
2 Mentally yell, "STOP!", then
3 Replace with positive thinking or your fondest memory, and then
4 In your mind's eye, see yourself taking charge in a relaxed, confident way.

BODY
1 Breathe in deeply, counting slowly up to 5, then
2 As you exhale completely, count slowly back to 1 and release all your muscles from head to toe, then
3 Imagine you are an old rag doll — loose, limp and relaxed. Use the directions for biofeedback.
4 Avoid caffeine, nicotine and other stress-packed chemicals. Instead, stretch or take a brisk walk.

Figure 11: Putting your key words on your *pocket guide*

For most activities, you might rehearse the day before, on the morning of the big day, and just before the event to visualize yourself taking charge in a relaxed, competent way.

What should you rehearse? You can mentally rehearse not only what you are going to do but also your approaches to stress relief.

For example, you might see yourself relaxing before you go in to give a presentation, focusing your thoughts on the task at hand, using healthy self-talk, making the presentation, giving yourself six-second tranquilizers to get through the tough parts, and then patting yourself mentally on the back when you have completed the activity.

"Instant Preplay"

This kind of previewing has been called "psychocybernetics" by some and "stress-inoculation" by others. The power of imagery techniques has been established scientifically.

If you don't have time to practice days or even hours in advance, try an "instant preplay." You can use these confidence-building techniques in many areas of your life to create peak performances in the boardroom, on the playing field, and at home with family members.

Improving Your Performance at the Moment of Truth

Instant preplay will prepare you for a performance, but what if you don't have time to practice or didn't practice enough? Even if you are fully prepared, you may find the next technique valuable.

When people perform, they often think about what could go wrong and how many important people are watching. These worries distract the mind just when full concentration is needed. We recommend asking yourself, "What must I *do*?"

This simple but powerful question will help you to stay fully focused on what you are doing. When you are focused, you optimize your performance and multiply the odds of success.

A Four-Step Technique for Mental Stress

On the *pocket guide* and in figure 12, we have condensed some of the best techniques in this section into a four-step routine for handling stress.

As one patient said just after the Chernobyl nuclear disaster, "When I use it early enough, I can prevent a mental meltdown."

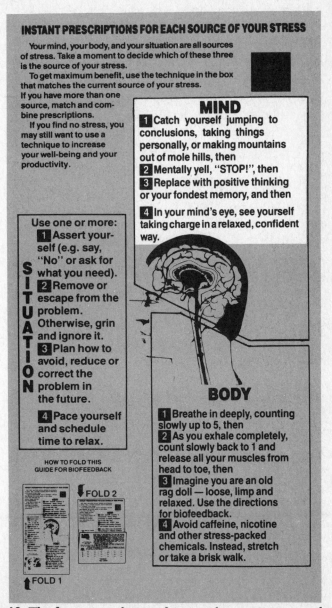

INSTANT PRESCRIPTIONS FOR EACH SOURCE OF YOUR STRESS

Your mind, your body, and your situation are all sources of stress. Take a moment to decide which of these three is the source of your stress.

To get maximum benefit, use the technique in the box that matches the current source of your stress. If you have more than one source, match and combine prescriptions.

If you find no stress, you may still want to use a technique to increase your well-being and your productivity.

MIND

1 Catch yourself jumping to conclusions, taking things personally, or making mountains out of mole hills, then

2 Mentally yell, "STOP!", then

3 Replace with positive thinking or your fondest memory, and then

4 In your mind's eye, see yourself taking charge in a relaxed, confident way.

SITUATION

Use one or more:

1 Assert yourself (e.g. say, "No" or ask for what you need).

2 Remove or escape from the problem. Otherwise, grin and ignore it.

3 Plan how to avoid, reduce or correct the problem in the future.

4 Pace yourself and schedule time to relax.

HOW TO FOLD THIS GUIDE FOR BIOFEEDBACK

FOLD 2

FOLD 1

BODY

1 Breathe in deeply, counting slowly up to 5, then

2 As you exhale completely, count slowly back to 1 and release all your muscles from head to toe, then

3 Imagine you are an old rag doll — loose, limp and relaxed. Use the directions for biofeedback.

4 Avoid caffeine, nicotine and other stress-packed chemicals. Instead, stretch or take a brisk walk.

Figure 12: The four-step technique for mental stress on your *pocket guide*

Using "Instant Replay" to Find What Pushed Your Buttons

The test you took and the instant stress test of the card may help you find the sources of your stress, but sometimes we are too involved to learn from our experience. It is often helpful to take a moment at the end of a stressful day and review it in your mind. Play back the film and look for the rough spots.

This "instant replay" can help you identify new areas where you need to apply stress-relief techniques. In combination with instant preplay, it can be a powerful way to prevent future stress.

Ten Prescriptions For Your Mind's Stress

FIVE TO TAKE THE STRESS OUT OF
WHAT YOU TELL YOURSELF

1. Catch yourself jumping to conclusions, taking things personally, or making mountains out of molehills.
2. Ask yourself, "Will it really matter five years from now?"
3. Challenge your unreasonable *shoulds, oughts, musts, owes,* and *deserves.*
4. Avoid exaggerated labels such as *stupid, lazy, dumb, crazy,* and *ugly.*
5. Use thought-stopping by mentally yelling, *Stop!,* seeing a red light, or hearing a whistle.

FIVE TO TURN ON THE POWER OF YOUR MIND
TO RELAX AND SUCCEED

1. Use images of your fondest memories and proudest moments to take vacations and overcome self-defeating emotions.
2. Become "stress-resistant" through commitment, control, and challenge.
3. Find health-enhancing phrases and repeat them regularly.
4. Laugh at yourself and the situation comedies around you.
5. Use "instant preplays" and "instant replays" to improve your performance.

V

Relieving the Stress of People and Situations

26

Taking the Stress Out of Your Surroundings

The stress in any situation involves the pressures and demands of both the people and the place. In this chapter, we will focus on the places where you live and work, so you can take the stress out of your surroundings.

Check Out Your Surroundings in a New Way

All too often we adjust to stressful conditions. If we are responding to other demands when we first experience minor irritants, we may learn to tune them out. Unfortunately, unpleasant surroundings can slowly erode the quality of our lives and leave us more vulnerable to other sources of stress.

Take a moment right now to scan the space around you. Use your five senses to detect any of these common stressful conditions:

1. Too much noise
2. Unpleasant odors
3. Uncomfortable furniture

157

4. Bad lighting
5. Poor ventilation

Consider Your Options

Once these conditions are identified, you have a number of options. For example, if the lighting is straining your eyes, you could find a different place to read, bring over another lamp, stop reading, or plan to correct the problem in the future. Each of these approaches can relieve stress by adding to your sense of comfort and control.

Even if you choose to ignore the problem, you will be aware of a genuine source of stress and you will be less likely to expend undue effort searching for other sources.

So, when you do a stress check during the day, be sure to consider your surroundings. For example, imagine that you are a salesperson talking with a customer in your office. Your fingers are cold. If you only check your body and your mind for stress, you might decide that you are nervous and try to warm your fingers. You would be expending a lot of energy and getting very little stress relief in return.

However, if you checked your surroundings, you might decide you are chilled because the air conditioning is too cold. Turning up the thermostat would be the obvious solution. By doing so, you would quickly and efficiently relieve stress for yourself and for your customer.

The message: Don't overlook the simple things.

If You Can't Remove the Stress in Your Surroundings

Many times you cannot remove the stress in your surroundings so easily. Most of us do not have total control over our surroundings; consequently, another option is simply to minimize your exposure to the stress. If the air conditioning in the above example is centrally controlled, for instance, the easiest thing might be to suggest a different meeting place.

Become Aware of the Clutter

When our surroundings are cluttered, we tend to feel over-whelmed because we are constantly reminded of future tasks. These reminders can interfere with concentration. If you keep only the current project and needed materials in view, you will feel more capable of success and your confidence will return.

The open office may not be the best place to get work done. When you are visible, you are far more open to interruption. In addition, just seeing others often adds to the input you process and aggravates information overload. If you work in an open office, consider rearranging your furniture so you face away from the line of sight.

At home, some of the same problems with privacy may arise. If they do, take action. Close doors, turn off the TV, and take the telephone off the hook for periods of time.

Be aware that stressful surroundings at one time of the day may create problems at a later time. High noise levels at work, for example, tend to disrupt sleep at night even if the place where you sleep is quiet.

Turning Down the Volume

Consider the modern office. Telephones ring, typewriters or printers clatter, and people talk loudly to be heard. Even without the sounds of occasional renovation or construction, it may be time to turn down the volume on the telephone and bring earplugs to work.

Consider escaping to a library or empty conference room for periods of time. Be sure to inform a secretary or co-worker of your whereabouts and on how to handle important calls.

Spring Cleaning for Stress

Some people have ignored so much for so long that they may need to take a few days to check their surroundings. Remember to use all your senses. Look, listen, touch, smell, and taste for stressful stimulation.

You may not be able to spend the time during the day to relieve the stress. Carry a small notepad and write down the stress sources you spot. Later, you can plan how to avoid, reduce, or correct the problem in the future. Just writing problems down and knowing you have set aside some time to plan modifications can help you regain a sense of control.

For now, let's look at ways to prevent some of the stress that comes from your surroundings.

27

Preventing Stress Where You Live and When You Travel

Most of the ideas we have presented in the last chapter involve reactive stress relief. Something is wrong, so we find the problem and fix it. But you can also reduce stress and optimize productivity by improving even livable surroundings. Small changes can pay daily dividends.

Taking the Stress Out of the Office

Consider your office. This time, let's look for improvements rather than earplugs and hideaways. Perhaps you can produce some renovation noise yourself by dividing the open spaces into rooms with thick carpets, putting up sound-absorbing walls or heavy drapes, and enclosing printers in foam-lined boxes.

Can you justify such changes? Point out that people who work in carpeted offices take fewer days off than those who work in vinyl-tiled offices.

Architectural psychologists now help design buildings to give visual relief from stress. Did you know that your eye muscles relax when you look at a far-distant view? Eye relaxation can create a pleasant ripple effect that will send relaxation throughout both your mind and body. Choose or plan buildings and windows to allow for such visual release.

Adjustable lighting can alleviate boredom. For this reason, sunlight is an excellent source of stimulation. Perhaps you can open blinds or choose rooms that take advantage of outside lighting.

Colors can be used to relieve stress or to provide stimulation. Muted pastels can calm; bright, primary colors can excite. Walls in emergency rooms and nursing homes are often painted accordingly.

You may not be in a position to choose a building or paint an office, but you can use pictures and lamps to create similar effects.

It is difficult to study the effects of these variables on productivity, but at least one medical study demonstrated that the view from a patient's room may help or hinder recovery. Patients who could see trees averaged shorter postoperative hospital stays, took less medication for pain relief, and suffered fewer postsurgical complications than those with a view of a brick wall. Consider these findings when you choose a hospital, too.

Home, Sweet Home

The needs of the home overlap somewhat with the office. For example, to prevent the stress of fires, make sure there are sufficient working smoke detectors, fire alarms, and extinguishers in your workplace and in your home. Know your exits. Conduct and participate in fire drills.

If you have limited control over one place where you spend time, you may want to compensate by making another setting truly outstanding. You probably have the most control at home.

Are you among the millions who now work at home? This situation often requires special stress relief. One couple, whose work involved home computer terminals, found themselves arguing constantly until the man set up his office on the top floor and the woman moved hers into the basement of their home.

Personal preferences should be indulged at home, but here are some general ideas to consider. First, you may want to free yourself of any excess baggage you have collected.

What's excess? Ask yourself if you have used something during the past year. If not, you might toss, sell, or store it elsewhere. Reviewing maintenance and insurance costs may provide the incentive to clear the clutter. Avoid burying yourself in the past, particularly if the memories upset you or interfere with your view of the future.

Consider improving your bedroom to make it more conducive to sleep. Create a dark, noiseless room with good ventilation. You may want to avoid the stress of an alarm or the morning news and awaken to an all-music radio station.

Many people find baths, showers, and hot tubs the best places for relaxation. If you do, pamper yourself. Pipe in music. Light candles. Buy the best towels you can afford.

Earlier, we discussed how to use your imagination to travel to personally relaxing places in your mind. You might also want to find a quiet retreat close to home, a special place where you can be alone with nature. Even in the city, sunrises, sunsets, and stars offer ways of gaining perspective and almost expanding time itself.

Television Tension

You may also want to take action against the major intruder of this century. In the average American home, the TV drones on for over seven hours a day.

Watching TV can be stressful. Distance was once a great buffer, but today we learn of economic downturns instantaneously and watch war from our living rooms.

Nearly half the main characters in TV dramas commit violence and over half are victims of it. Surveys suggest that heavy viewers see themselves as living in a hostile world. Fortunately, situation comedies are the most popular programs.

However, unless the tube is merely a substitute for the fireplace of old, TV can disrupt family communication and activities. Imposing time limits or moving the TV to a new location may open up healthier options.

Easing the Stress of Commuting

Buckling your seat belt is one of the easiest and most important ways to avoid or to reduce major situational stress instantly. Unless you have worked in a hospital or a funeral home, you probably don't realize how much stress you can prevent for yourself and your family.

For Americans under the age of forty-four, automobile accidents are the leading cause of death. Granted, the likelihood of an accident on any one trip is low, but your lifetime odds of a serious accident are over 30 percent.

Numerous studies have shown that wearing a seat belt at least doubles your chances of escaping serious injury or death in a major automobile accident. So, buckle up and perform a death-defying act every time you enter an automobile.

Many people think seat belts contribute to a lot of deaths and use that notion as an excuse to take their chances. Do you know the odds of dying in a car wreck while wearing a belt? Of 649 people who died in auto accidents in 1983 in Colorado, only 7 were wearing seat belts.

Half the states in the United States now have mandatory seat belt laws. In the first year of enforcement of New York's seat belt law, the number of automobile deaths declined to the state's lowest level since 1949. It is estimated that nearly 90 percent of all infant deaths and 75 percent of all infant injuries could be prevented by proper use of car seats.

Why the hard sell? Unfortunately, fewer than one in five Americans use seat belts regularly.

Make buckling up as much a habit as putting the key in the ignition. If you forget, buckle up and drive back to where you forgot. The retracing is as foolish as forgetting, but after a few of these double trips, you will be more likely to remember to wear your seat belt.

Relieving the Stress While Keeping Your Eyes on the Road

Your eyes are very sensitive to light, and too much sunlight can sap your energy. Carry sunglasses in your car. In addition, choose different routes to fulfill different needs.

Most of us only consider time and distance when choosing a route. However, a study of train commuters showed that those boarding only twenty miles from the city actually produced more adrenaline than those traveling twice the distance. Scenery, safety, crowding, control, and other variables can also be important sources of stress and relief.

Most of us spend more time in the car than we realize. Improvements can be as inexpensive as cleaning out your car or as expensive as buying a new one that is equipped with a stereo tape deck for your favorite music or educational cassettes.

Stress Relief for the Traveler

When you leave home, anticipate and select your surroundings. To breathe the cleanest air on a plane, ask your booking agent or boarding clerk for a seat in the middle of the nonsmoking section. If you want to avoid children, let your agent or clerk know your preference. If you are tall or easily cramped, ask for a seat behind a compartment wall, in line with an exit, near a service area, or on an aisle, so you can stretch your legs.

When you travel to a different climate, your body does not have time to adapt by changing the amount of water in your blood. The more extreme the weather change, the greater the stress of keeping your body's temperature in the normal range.

Even at home, rapid fluctuations are stressful enough that weather reports in some areas now give a "weather-stress index." Bringing enough clothes of different weights for layering and removal can relieve this stress near home and on the road.

You might also want to bring a favorite pillow to help you sleep. Once again, it's often the small things that can quickly take the edge off stress.

Shared Surroundings Can Be Stressful

To improve some of the places where you work, play, and travel, you may need more privacy to avoid the stress of overcrowding. If this cannot be arranged, you may need to ask others to change.

When you are stressed by someone's smoke, loud music, interruptions, or temperature preferences, you have a people problem as much as a place problem.

In upcoming chapters, you will find ways to communicate and negotiate with others quickly and firmly.

28

Communicating Assertively for Stress Relief

M ost people can become more readily aware of the stress in their surroundings. If alone, they can usually do something to reduce or remove the irritants of stress. The more challenging situational stress usually comes from our interactions with other people.

Look back to chapter 6 and find those items you marked 3, 4, or 5 on the Stress in Your Situation Scale. Most of these probably involve other people and could be improved through more effective communication.

Pick one of the items and a specific situation to think about as you read the next section.

The Stress of Communicating

Communicating is one of man's great accomplishments, but it is stressful. The act of talking raises blood pressure and heart rate. Research shows these changes occur even among the deaf when they sign.

Psychologists have identified three styles of communicating: passive, assertive, and aggressive. Both passive and aggressive communicating *seem* to relieve stress instantly but really burden the user with long-term distress.

The Inward Flight of Passive Behavior

When we are passive, we try to please others and bury our needs. We make no demands on others. They are free to do as they wish and all conflict is avoided. We have taken an inward flight from the situation, and the stress of the moment seems instantly relieved.

Think of your stressful situation. Were you passive when you communicated with the other person? Perhaps you decided not to bring up the problem and remained silent when you could have spoken.

By being passive, we often invite others to take advantage of us. If this happens, we may stockpile anger and suffer in silence. We may agree to do too much and procrastinate on things we never really wanted to do.

The Disruptive Fight of Aggressive Behavior

When we are aggressive, we bully others and step on their rights in an attempt to protect our own. Threats and putdowns may get us what we want and relieve our stress in the short run, but the long-term effects of these disruptive fights can be harmful.

Think again about your stressful situation. Were you angry? Perhaps you felt good getting it off your chest. Letting off steam occasionally is healthy, but it is often followed by feelings of guilt and loneliness. In addition, there is growing evidence that chronic hostility and cynicism may multiply the chances of developing heart disease and dying prematurely.

Anger may be related to heart disease because of what anger does to our relationships with others. After a fight, others are likely to feel tense and resentful. After repeated fights, we may lose our social network and have no one to turn to when things go wrong.

The Assertive Alternative

Assertive behavior is a big improvement over the instinctive fight-or-flight response of the cave dweller. It is also the best alternative to the stress of a disruptive fight or an inward flight in modern life.

Assertiveness involves clear, direct, honest, and firm communication of what we want and how we feel. It takes time to learn if most of our communications have been either passive or aggressive. However, once learned, assertive techniques can be used just as instantaneously as passive or aggressive ones.

Assertiveness is the use of personal power in a positive and pleasant way. It typically adds to our self-confidence, earns us respect, and increases our odds of winning.

Could you have been assertive in your stressful situation? How would you have acted? What might have been the outcome?

In the next chapter you will learn how one of our patients asked for a raise and got it through assertiveness.

29

Asking for a Raise with Assertiveness

Joan worked for a large advertising firm. She was the administrative secretary for an account manager named Bill until he left. Over the following three months, Joan gradually took over most of his duties but also began suffering daily headaches.

Her boss, Bob, was very pleased with her work, but Joan was angry. Account managers averaged $800 a week and she still took home $400.

Joan asked for a raise in three different ways. Before she learned assertiveness, she was very passive. It took Joan a month to decide finally to talk with her rather intimidating boss. All morning, between phone calls, Joan had been thinking about what she had decided to do.

A Passive Approach

At 11:45 she went to Don's office, hoping to catch him before lunch. She knocked and entered to find Don hurrying to put some papers into his briefcase. Joan nervously cleared her throat and asked, "Is this a good time to talk?" Without waiting for an answer, she added cautiously, "Ah, you look a little rushed."

Don, still shuffling his papers, said, "Not the best, but what can I do for you?"

"Maybe I should come back another time," Joan asked, not knowing if she wanted him to say yes or no.

Don quickly answered, "No, I'm booked the rest of the day."

Joan looked down at the floor and stammered, "Well, I, ah, I've been thinking that since I'm, well, you know, doing a lot of what Bill did before he left, that, ah, maybe you could give me a raise."

Don checked his watch and said hurriedly, "You've been doing a super job, but you know, things are tight now. That's why we can't replace Bill. Look, I've got a lunch meeting with the Jackson account. Maybe we can talk about this another time. I'm sure we can work something out."

When Joan came in for help, she was using aspirin daily to relieve her tension headaches. After five weeks of biofeedback-assisted relaxation training and home practice with progressive relaxation, she reported only one headache the week before. Then she announced she was thinking about quitting her job.

An Aggressive Approach

Asked to explain, she shared the fantasy of storming into Don's office and saying, "I hate working here. If you don't give me a $100 raise, I'm quitting. In fact, you've been discriminating against me because I'm a woman and I'm going to sue you and this company. Don't tell me we'll work something out because you've had your chance. You can take your job and shove it."

Joan didn't really want to quit her job; she wanted to know how to deal with the situation and she wanted a raise. During assertiveness training, Joan first "preplayed" and then successfully dealt with several other situations in which she had less to lose. Next, she carefully planned, "preplayed," and role-played her encounter with Don.

An Assertive Approach

Joan managed the situation very differently this time. She requested an appointment with Don to discuss her new position. When asked what she wanted, Joan repeated her request for an appointment when they could be free of distractions.

Just before the appointment, Joan relaxed, using the deep-breathing technique. She also cleared her mind with some humor by remembering that even bosses use toilets. As a result, Joan walked into Don's office confidently.

Rather than accusing or begging, she thanked him for meeting with her and said, "As you know, since Bill left, I have taken over his duties as account manager. I am contributing more and I would like to discuss a new salary for my new position."

Don looked at her. Joan looked back at him attentively. She used silence to allow Don to make a decision. Don waited, then said, "Well, the most I can get you is $600."

This was twice the raise Joan had hoped for. Knowing that might happen, her therapist had helped her practice several responses, including the one she gave. Joan admitted later that she had felt like falling out of her seat or gushing "thank you's" as if he had given her a gift. But she managed to thank him and even asked, "Would it be possible to reevaluate my work in six months to see if I am contributing as much as managers hired from outside the firm?"

Don's expression was one of surprise, but his "yes" reflected a growing respect for the firm's new, assertive manager.

30

Recognizing Assertiveness

Entire books and courses are devoted to assertiveness training. However, the first step toward becoming less aggressive or passive and more assertive involves recognizing these three types of behavior in yourself and in others.

Using the chart below, you may want to review the example you just read and begin categorizing the communication styles of other people. Try imagining how the aggressive or passive communications you see could have been made more assertively.

You may also want to use the chart and the Stress in Your Situation Scale to think about how you are handling each interpersonal item you marked 3, 4, or 5 on the scale.

Consider your previous actions and future options, but do not change your behavior until you have learned some techniques here or elsewhere. Once you know what to do, proceed slowly. Start by gaining confidence and skill in less important situations. The biggest mistake people make in learning assertiveness is trying it first on their bosses or spouses.

Three Communication Styles

The Passive Style

A person using the passive style of communicating:

1. Allows others to choose when, where, and what will happen
2. Avoids saying what he or she wants or feels
3. Asks to be turned down with such expressions as, *If you wouldn't mind . . .*
4. Gives up if the first request is refused
5. Uses such empty phrases as *you know* or *I mean*
6. Hides real feelings to avoid disagreements
7. Uses many vague words hoping to be understood
8. Manipulates through a helpless, "poor me" attitude
9. Criticizes what he or she does and apologizes often
10. Cowers in posture, voice, and manner

The Aggressive Style

A person using the aggressive style of communicating:

1. Uses the word "You" to send messages that hurt, accuse, or blame
2. Uses threats, labels, and putdowns
3. Sets up "win–lose" situations rather than negotiating
4. "Ambushes" people when they are unprepared or preoccupied
5. Listens little or only to what he or she wants to hear
6. Exaggerates with such words as *always* or *never*
7. Manipulates and chooses for others
8. Uses one-upmanship
9. Intimidates others with an exaggerated show of power
10. Threatens others in posture, voice, and manner

The Assertive Style

A person using the assertive style of communicating:

1. Uses the word *I*, showing ownership of feelings and needs
2. Negotiates clearly and directly for what is wanted
3. Leans forward in a relaxed manner and makes eye contact
4. Makes references to specific behaviors
5. Uses active listening to find a "win–win" solution
6. Sets a convenient time to discuss or negotiate things
7. Sets a firm time and follows up to avoid being put off
8. Avoids exaggerating with words such as *always* or *never*
9. Keeps the communication short and simple
10. Calmly repeats appropriate requests

The next chapter will focus on three of the shortest and most powerful assertive techniques for instant stress relief.

31

Three Powerful Assertive Techniques for Instant Stress Relief

Two-Letter Stress Relief: The Word *No*

If you find that you are always behind and frustrated by too many things to do, start using the word no. This magic two-letter word can give you instant stress relief.

No can help you avoid trying to be all things to all people. Use it frequently, and it can give you the time to do the things you really want to do.

Saying yes when it would be best to say no increases the likelihood that the other person will ask again and ask for more. With some people this cycle can escalate until a very lopsided relationship exists. There may be a giver and a taker rather than a balance of give and take.

If in many relationships you are the giver, the stress can be overwhelming. Don't blame the other people in these relationships. Take the responsibility to say no.

No is more honest than saying yes and procrastinating. *No* also encourages the other person to seek other solutions to his or her problem. If we do what others are capable of doing or of learn-

176

ing to do for themselves, we foster unhealthy dependency. Rather than giving, we are taking away another's opportunities for self-sufficiency.

You have the right to refuse requests. In fact, if you never say no, your yesses don't mean very much.

One of our patients called herself a Type E—she was trying to be everything to everyone. She taught so many people to depend on her help that it was taken for granted. A combination of resentment and exhaustion led to migrainelike headaches. Refusing requests took courage, but saying no was a turning point on her journey back to health.

If some people you know just will not take no for an answer, you may need to use the next technique and calmly repeat the word until they stop asking.

The Broken-Record Technique

One of the authors asked to be called after his car was tuned up and the battery replaced. When he went to pick up his car, it would not start.

The clerk admitted that a mistake had been made and the battery had not been replaced, but he said that it would be an hour or more before a mechanic could install a new one.

The author really needed instant stress relief. He used his cue word, *relax*, for a six-second tranquilizer, cleared his mind of homicidal thoughts, and calmly said, "I don't want to wait an hour. I want you to replace the battery now." The clerk said, "You will just have to wait like everyone else, buddy."

The author's ride back to his office was gone. Time for the broken record technique. The author calmed himself once again and said, "I asked to be called when my car was ready. It's not ready and I want you to replace the battery now."

When the clerk refused, the author asked to see the manager. Told that there was no manager, he asked to see the person in charge.

The author repeated the request to the supervisor twice before he was sent to see Joe, the mechanic. "Joe, I asked to be called when my car was ready. I was called, but it is not ready because they forgot to tell you to replace the battery. Would you please replace it now?" said the author.

Joe replied, "We are swamped, can't you wait?"

The answer, of course, was, "I asked to be called when my car was ready, would you please put the battery in now?" Joe called to another mechanic, "Throw a battery in this guy's car."

Persistence pays. In fact, according to *Boardroom Reports*, "Of all new sales, 80 percent are made after the fifth sales call."

Calmly repeating your request like a broken record does not guarantee success, but it does increase your odds and decrease your stress.

The Power of Silence

When you have made a request, a brief period of silence can yield many rewards. It is a good time to use your cue word for some instant relaxation and it gives the other person some time to make a decision.

If you fill up the silence, you may invite the other person to refuse your request. For example, some people will ask for something and then say, "Well, it really isn't that important," or "Maybe I shouldn't have asked, but . . ."

A salesperson we know went so far as to say, "After I make a sales presentation, I always ask for the order, but then I shut up. The first one to talk loses." He explained that if he talks, he is likely to cut his commission by offering another discount. If he lets the customer talk, he either gets the order or learns the reasons why the customer is reluctant to buy.

Whether in a business or a social situation, a relaxed silence can communicate confident expectations. People tend to do what they feel is expected of them. If we make reasonable requests in effective ways, we are more likely to get our needs met and to decrease our stress.

Did you find these techniques helpful? You may want to read some of the books or listen to some of the recordings about assertiveness listed in appendix II.

The three tools of *The One Minute Manager*—one-minute goal setting, praising, and reprimanding—are all excellent, assertive ways of relieving stress in the workplace. We highly recommend the book and tapes of that title listed in the appendix. If you are a parent, you might also consider *The One Minute Father* or *The One Minute Mother*.

Assertiveness training is available in most large communities. Group training is often most effective because you can role-play, get feedback, and learn how others use assertiveness. Ask your physician or mental health professional for more information about individual or group therapy.

32

Instant Ways to Manage Time

Time can be an enemy or a friend, depending on how you use it. If you agree to do too much in too little time, the days of your life will be spent in a never-ending fight or flight against the clock. If you know what you want and move gradually toward fulfilling goals, you will enjoy the journey.

The use of time involves an endless series of decisions, big and small, that gradually shape our lives. Instant ways to manage time are powerful, but they are most helpful in making the small decisions.

Before presenting instant ways of managing time, we want to encourage you to write down your life goals—the results of your big decisions. If you cannot list them in the time it takes to make instant rice, you may not know what you want out of life. The lack of clear goals may be a major source of your stress.

Choosing Your Goals and Planning Your Life

To start relieving that stress, you will need to make time to plan your life. Unfortunately, if you are like most people, you have probably spent more time planning a vacation than planning your life.

Time-management books and courses will help you set goals and priorities better than we can here. However, be sure that you write down not only your lifelong goals but also the goals you would choose if the next six months were to be the last six months of your life. Such an approach helps you focus on what is most important and how to avoid living for the "someday" you may never see.

Strive to simplify your life. When your calendar looks crowded, it often reflects a lack of goal-setting. Focus on your strongest interests, deepest values, and greatest talents. Knowing what you want will allow you to do fewer things better and more of the things you truly enjoy.

If you have narrowed your goals, but a goal for the day or for the year still seems too big, break it into smaller ones. Remember, "You can eat an elephant—one bite at a time."

The Night Before, Write Your To-Do Lists

Once your goals are broken into manageable chunks, take time each night to write down what you want to accomplish the next day. Sleep often yields creative solutions. If you assign tasks to others near closing time, they too may get fresh ideas overnight.

This strategy works well for most situations, but there are exceptions. One dentist who always laid out his instruments for the next day's work before leaving the office at night found himself waking up early and thinking through each operation rather than going back to sleep. The instant stress relief came when he began asking his staff to prepare the instruments but not tell him the work scheduled for the next day.

Take the Time to Plan Your Day

Once you have your to-do list, sort it into those activities requiring your prime time, "fillers" for time between major activities, things you enjoy doing, jobs you dislike, and tasks you can delegate.

Set aside your most productive hours for your most important tasks. During this prime time, arrange to have your calls screened by a secretary, an answering machine, or a co-worker with whom you alternate.

To avoid procrastination and relieve stress, schedule the work you dislike before the activities you enjoy and vary the content of your work.

If you also schedule time to make brief follow-up calls to check on progress, delegated work is more likely to be completed on time and by the right person. Use this approach and you will avoid the stress of what some executives call last-minute "reverse delegation."

Time for Yourself

Schedule time for several brief relaxation breaks. By planning more breaks than you need, you will ensure that you will also have a little more time for the unexpected.

If you have children, you may want to arrange times for short but daily phone contacts from work. What a great way to give and get instant stress relief!

To avoid burnout, eat lunch away from the office with old friends in new places. Attend meetings so you can get off the treadmill and gain perspective.

Develop a daily decompression routine to give you a break between the duties you have at work and home. It might be reading a paper, driving through a park, or window shopping. If you must go home immediately, train your family to give you at least ten minutes for decompression upon arrival.

Time for Fun

Try scheduling at least one pleasurable mini-event each day, something you really enjoy. Mini-events, even if demanding, can be energizing and stress relieving. Just be sure to use different parts of your body, mind, or surroundings.

Plan your weekends and evenings at least as carefully as your workdays, so you can make the most of your friendships and family life.

Should all this scheduling sound too rigid, plan some time for spontaneity. It could be an hour or a day to do whatever you want to do on impulse. We all need time to nurture and to enjoy the child within us. By setting clear goals and knowing when you will accomplish them, you avoid guilt or anxiety about using other time to give yourself pleasure.

If you learned that work is good, but no one ever told you how much and no one encouraged you to play and rest, it is easy to become a workaholic. It may help to think of the butterfly basking in the sun. Perhaps their sunning looks unnecessary or even wasteful, but butterflies must absorb enough heat to raise their internal temperature before they can fly. If you wish to succeed, you, too, must "fuel up" with rest and relaxation.

Schedule Enough Time for Sleep

We spend about a third of our lives sleeping. Studies show that those who sleep seven to eight hours a night live longer and enjoy better health, on the average, than those who sleep more or fewer hours. However, different people have different needs.

You may want to experiment for about a week with a given retiring and rising time and see how you feel. Then try a different "dose" each week for a month.

During periods of major stress, you may need to "sleep on it." A good night's sleep often brings a new perspective and the energy to solve problems.

When scheduling for sleep, leave ample time to slow your pace before you go to bed. Following a nightly routine can condition the body to sleep. Don't allow yourself to toss and turn for more than about ten minutes. By getting up, you avoid making the bed a cue for wakefulness and worry. Alcohol and over-the-counter aids for insomnia disrupt sleep and should be avoided in favor of relaxation techniques.

Schedule Less Time in Stressful Situations

If you know certain situations are stressful and evoke time-urgency, hostility, or any other unpleasant emotion, try scheduling less time in those settings. Many but not all of these are work situations. Also, try spending less time with people who are angry, intimidating, or pessimistic.

One of our patients suffered stress visiting her aging father, because he criticized her and used guilt to extend the length of her visits. By scheduling her visits fifteen minutes before she needed to go to work and changing what she told herself about his comments, she minimized her stressful exposure to the situation, while still visiting him daily.

The Power of "Not-to-Do" Lists

Some common time robbers are extended phone calls, unnecessary interruptions, lengthy meetings, unimportant paperwork, and meaningless television shows. The unpleasant or unproductive can go on an instant "not-to-do" list. Others can be added by carefully reviewing an average day in ten-minute segments to see what you would like to eliminate.

Check your not-to-do list for time robbers when you look at your to-do list for new tasks. Eliminate or reduce one or two robbers on your most unwanted list every day. You will find that the more you respect your time, the more others will respect it.

Relieving the Stress of Interruptions and Lengthy Meetings

Keep an interruption log to learn what kinds of problems are presented by whom and when. Many interruptions are necessary. Others can be reduced or eliminated. The log may help you decide to ask people to keep a list of their own concerns, as well as possible solutions, and to schedule a daily meeting to help them make final decisions.

If you find people use your office as an informal meeting place, you may be able to discourage this activity by limiting the number of chairs available. A visible clock also tends to shorten interruptions. Standing during or at the end of interruptions can also keep them brief and productive.

If you want to see another person but only for a few minutes, offer to meet in his or her office. It is easier to excuse yourself from another person's office than to ask someone to leave yours.

When you return or receive a call and you want to keep it short, avoid asking "How are you?" Say hello and ask, "What can I do for you?" Returning calls a little before lunch or near closing time may also keep them short.

If someone on the phone or in your office is longwinded, listen for the most important issue, summarize it, and suggest a solution, another appointment, or someone else the person might ask. Find ways to end a conversation comfortably; become aware of how others do this. Adapt their approaches to your style and begin using some of them to relieve the stress of time instantly in a variety of situations.

33

Relieving Loneliness and the Stress Others Create for You

Supportive family and friends are buffers against stress. Studies of large groups of people have shown that, regardless of prior illnesses, those with few close contacts die two to three times sooner than those who confide in others regularly.

There is nothing instant about deep relationships, but you can nurture them in many small ways and preserve them by quickly relieving the stress they inevitably create.

Where Is Everyone?

Human and animal research clearly support the importance of building close friendships and of deepening family relationships. However, there are fewer extended families and close-knit small-town communities today.

On the other hand, the growth and diversity of self-help groups and clubs offer opportunities for developing the social support you may need. Work, volunteer activities, and religious gatherings can also be sources for people with whom you can nurture friendships.

Reach Out and Touch Someone

Don't wait for others to reach out. Relax your mind and body, take a small risk relative to the pain of loneliness, and make the first move. Set clear goals, such as introducing yourself to at least one new person each week or inviting friends over every weekend.

Often we take loved ones for granted and focus on their faults. To increase your appreciation and tolerance for those closest to you, treat them as if each day were the last day of their lives.

If you have trouble expressing your love, use "instant preplay" to practice and then do it. The benefits are worth the risks.

All living creatures need to touch and be touched. Hugs and kisses have been studied and recommended by both poets and scientists. Relaxation can enhance all forms of touch.

Busy partners may find it best to plan times for intimacy. Romance may actually be heightened by anticipation. With enough time, you can teach each other what is most pleasurable and make love lazily.

How Our Expectations and Fears Create Conflict

When we discussed the mind as a source of stress, we showed how exaggerated thoughts led to exaggerated feelings. Most of our thoughts come from what we were taught as children by our families.

Marriage and friendships involve people from different families with different expectations and divergent interpretations of what people do.

These differing expectations and interpretations lead to misunderstandings and conflict. For example, what if someone starts staying late at work more often? Does this mean that the person is more committed to a family, or less? Do the longer hours reflect a fear of poverty, an attraction to a co-worker, or some other possibility?

Jumping to conclusions often creates conflict, and open communication frequently relieves stress.

Get More Information

One of the keys to relieving stress at home or work is asking for more information without accusing the other person. It is very important to use calm assertiveness and "I" messages. For example, "I'm confused, could you tell me why you are staying late?" or "I'm feeling unhappy about this, how many nights will you be away?" The important thing is to get more information.

The same is true when you handle criticism. Use your relaxation skills, focus on what you can learn from the situation, and ask how you could do it better next time. If you disagree with the new approach, avoid opposing it head-on. It may be best to argue for still a third approach or a compromise.

Give More Information

It is equally important to give others feedback and information so that misunderstandings can be avoided. This takes courage. The stress and suspense in most soap operas is based on the lack of shared information. Open communications can keep your life from becoming a soap opera of misunderstandings.

While telling others about what you think and feel is important, you do not have to answer every question. Sometimes it is best to challenge the basis for the question, change the subject, or ask a question yourself. All of these techniques can slow things down and give you more information about the question.

Handling Anger and Other Strong Emotions

If someone is angry, don't take it personally. There are too many possible reasons for the anger to begin doubting yourself. Focus on the task at hand and ask for help. If the anger is still getting in the way, you have several options.

Following are four instant ways to relieve the stress of someone else's anger. You can also use the same techniques to respond to other strong emotions.

1. **Be assertive.** To review, your goal is to be clear, honest, direct, and firm. You might try, "When you yell like that, I get upset and I can't concentrate on what we are doing."

2. **Listen actively.** Point out the anger and ask what triggered it. You might try, "You sound angry. What are you angry about?" If you think *angry* is too strong, you might try *upset*.

When you point out another person's feelings in a tentative, nonjudgmental way, you buy a little time and help the person regain composure.

Just the label you give the emotion often helps the other person feel understood. In addition, if the person tells you what the anger is about, you may learn that it has nothing to do with you or what you did to arouse the anger.

3. **Ignore the anger.** Sometimes it is best just to let the person cool off. To avoid jumping into the fray, focus on changing your self-talk.

The danger with ignoring is ignorance. It prevents you from learning about the problem. Getting more information could help you improve the situation or find ways of dealing with similar problems in the future.

4. **Escape from the situation.** If your presence is not required, just walk away. This approach has some of the same disadvantages as ignoring the problem. Once out of the situation, you may be able to find another way to handle the conflict and return to deal with it more effectively the next time.

There are many wonderful bosses. There are also some from whom it might be best to escape. A recent survey identified a few of the more difficult bosses. Is your boss a backbiting "snake-in-the-grass," an easily threatened "little Napoleon," a humiliating "heel grinder," a know-it-all "egotist," or a go-by-the-book "detail drone"?

Sometimes we stay in a job situation too long. A bad worker–boss or person–job fit can be as stressful as a bad marriage, and sometimes you need to get a divorce. However, the best time to find a new job is when you have one, so hang in there until you have found a better job.

If you repeatedly get into emotionally draining entanglements and situations that always go sour, ask yourself what attracted you to the people and the jobs in the first place. If you need professional help figuring out the pattern, get some. With hard work, most patterns can be interrupted and major stress avoided.

Brief Lists of Situational Relief Techniques

In figure 13, we have condensed some of the best techniques in this section for quick reference on the *pocket guide*. You can also find these and others at the end of this chapter on a list of ten prescriptions for your situational stress.

Sounds Great, But I Can't See Myself Doing That

If you like some of the suggestions in this chapter but keep backing off from using them, your source of stress may be a combination of mind and situation.

You may be telling yourself that if you are assertive, people won't like you. Or that if you take control of your time, people will think you're selfish. Or if you reach out, others will only reject you. These thoughts can be immobilizing, but they can also be changed. Here is an example.

Andy, a safety engineer we treated, suffered from burnout. We reviewed his work situation at a nuclear reactor and began treatment by recommending that he take his coffee and lunch breaks. Andy agreed that breaks were important, but he returned the next week to say he just couldn't take them.

We asked Andy why and discovered the belief that kept him from taking his breaks. A young and dedicated engineer, Andy feared that something would happen to the reactor when he was on break. He would never be able to forgive himself if it leaked radiation.

Another engineer was available to take over during breaks, but Andy was too afraid to leave. We asked him what happened when he was at home the other sixteen hours of the day. The answer was obvious but it was the beginning of recovery.

It took hard work, but by relaxing and reminding himself that he took the same risk when he was away from work, he was able to start taking his breaks and relieving his stress.

Many people want to take vacations or to be more assertive, but

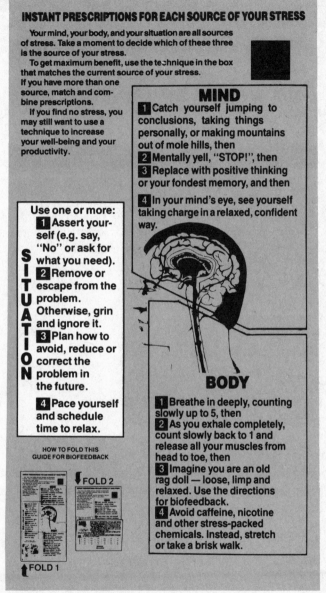

INSTANT PRESCRIPTIONS FOR EACH SOURCE OF YOUR STRESS

Your mind, your body, and your situation are all sources of stress. Take a moment to decide which of these three is the source of your stress.

To get maximum benefit, use the technique in the box that matches the current source of your stress.

If you have more than one source, match and combine prescriptions.

If you find no stress, you may still want to use a technique to increase your well-being and your productivity.

MIND

1 Catch yourself jumping to conclusions, taking things personally, or making mountains out of mole hills, then

2 Mentally yell, "STOP!", then

3 Replace with positive thinking or your fondest memory, and then

4 In your mind's eye, see yourself taking charge in a relaxed, confident way.

SITUATION

Use one or more:

1 Assert yourself (e.g. say, "No" or ask for what you need).

2 Remove or escape from the problem. Otherwise, grin and ignore it.

3 Plan how to avoid, reduce or correct the problem in the future.

4 Pace yourself and schedule time to relax.

HOW TO FOLD THIS GUIDE FOR BIOFEEDBACK

BODY

1 Breathe in deeply, counting slowly up to 5, then

2 As you exhale completely, count slowly back to 1 and release all your muscles from head to toe, then

3 Imagine you are an old rag doll — loose, limp and relaxed. Use the directions for biofeedback.

4 Avoid caffeine, nicotine and other stress-packed chemicals. Instead, stretch or take a brisk walk.

FOLD 2

FOLD 1

Figure 13: Situational stress relief on the *pocket guide*.

they say, "I just can't see myself doing that." *Seeing* yourself relieve stress with the techniques in this section may be just what's needed. Use your imagination to see yourself delegating or taking charge. If you have trouble believing in yourself, remember: Seeing is believing.

Alter, Avoid, or Accept Situations

Some situations cannot be modified or sidestepped. There *are* human problems that defy solution. In such cases, we need to recognize our limits.

If a situation cannot be altered or avoided, we need to accept it. Accepting often involves letting go and changing our expectations by using relief strategies for the body and mind.

That is the sort of flexibility the system you are learning offers. The next and final section will show you additional ways of choosing and combining techniques for instant stress relief.

Ten Prescriptions for Handling Your Situational Stress

1. Make healthy changes in your surroundings to remove or reduce stressful noise, odors, objects, and lighting.
2. Use seat belts.
3. Ask assertively for what you need.
4. Say no to stressful requests.
5. Use the broken-record technique and calmly repeat your requests.
6. Communicate with silence, so as to avoid talking yourself out of what you need.
7. Schedule less time in stressful situations and escape from them, if possible.
8. Manage time so as to get enough relaxation, recreation, and sleep.
9. Listen actively to clarify and to improve emotional situations.
10. Reach out to meet and to get close to others.

Putting
It All
Together

34

Scanning Sets the Stage for Instant Stress Relief

In the daily drama of life, you may find your body full of stage fright, your lines and emotions out of control, or the performance schedule much too tight. You know the sources of stress and ways to find instant relief. Now it is time to put it all together and use the full system.

Scanning for Stress

To obtain maximum benefit from the techniques we have described, you will need to make scanning a habit. As you move through each scene in your day, you will want to scan your body, mind, and situation to find sources of stress.

Scanning is important because it sets the stage for instant stress relief. Once you find a source, you can match and use one of the techniques you learned for that source.

You may find it helpful to write the word SCAN on transparent tape and put it over the crystal on your watch or on a clock you look at several times a day. You may also want to stick the word on your

195

refrigerator door, the dashboard of your car, and your telephones. The goal is to remind yourself twenty to thirty times a day to scan and to relieve your stress.

Many people use a six-second relaxation response whenever they scan. The relaxation seems to help them to think more clearly about the sources of stress. You may want to use your key word as a reminder both to relax and scan throughout the day.

The Best Scanning Sequence

We are often asked to order the three sources of stress from most to least important as a guide to optimal scanning and relief. The best order varies from person to person, however.

You may want to order the sources according to your scores on the Seven-Minute Stress Test. Start with the source that has the highest percentile score and end with the one that has the lowest. That would bring your attention right away to the areas you most often find stressful.

The best order also depends on your goals. If your goal is to prevent stress-related disease, then checking your body first will help you determine if you are overreacting physically to any of the sources of stress. If your goal is to feel happy, you might check your mind first. If your goal is overcoming stress to boost productivity, you might first scan your situation.

Finding Your Firing Order

Still another approach to picking the best scanning sequence involves finding what some have called your "firing order."

If you look back at the times you have been most stressed and write down the order of your responses, you can usually detect a pattern. This pattern may help you work on a specific stress. It may also suggest the best order for ongoing, daily scanning.

Take George, a fifty-five-year-old accountant who, after bypass surgery, had complaints of confusion, dizziness, sleeping problems, and loss of confidence. By describing a typical episode, he became aware of his firing order, discovered a useful scanning sequence, and pointed the way toward the best interventions for his problems.

Whenever George and his wife had accepted an invitation to a social event or business party, his symptoms would increase.

First, he would think about what he called the "devastating" surgery. He would remind himself, "I'll never be the same." Then George would imagine how he might forget someone's name or spill a drink. At that point, George would start to feel dizzy, his heart would race, and he would tell his wife to cancel the invitation.

George's firing order was mind, body, and situation. He learned to scan and to use his stress relief strategies in that order.

For example, he learned to scan his mind first and replaced *devastating* with either *lifesaving* or *unpleasant*. *I'll never be the same* became *It may be slow, but I'm making progress*, or *I wasn't goof-proof before, either*. Next, George rehearsed confident images of an imperfect but very pleasant evening.

George then focused on his body and used relaxation techniques to change tense apprehension into calm anticipation. Finally, turning to the situational sources of stress, he began selecting progressively more demanding social events rather than accepting invitations indiscriminately.

During social events, George would scan and relieve stress in the same order: mind, body, and situation. In a few months, George had renewed his social life and his self-confidence.

A Common Scanning Recipe

The most common order for scanning is probably body, mind, and then situation. If you choose this order, you might scan for tension in your muscles and then either place your thumb on the *pocket guide* to take the quick test or place your hand on your neck to check for coolness. You might also scan for a rapid pulse, nervous sweating, or shallow breathing. Any of these could indicate stress in your body.

Next, you will shift your attention and scan your mind for any worrisome, unproductive thoughts; frightening, exaggerated images; or the disruptive, upsetting feelings they evoke.

You will register your findings and move right on to scanning your situation for stressful demands from people or distressful inputs from your surroundings. Most of us are very much aware of what we are doing and what is going on around us, so this final step can be done very rapidly.

Once you have scanned, it is time to choose the best technique for the sources you have identified. For a while, you may need to jog your memory by consulting the ten prescriptions at the end of each relief section or the inner side of the *pocket guide*. The *guide* also serves as a cue to scan, so keep it with you in a pocket or purse.

The next chapter will help you choose and combine techniques to maximize your stress relief.

35

Choosing and Combining Prescriptions for Peak Performance

The instant stress-relief system is a flexible way to enhance your health, productivity, and enjoyment of life. Once you have scanned, you can match one or more techniques for each source of stress you find.

Are You Really Ready?

One of the things you must take into consideration when you choose the best technique is your ability to use it and the risk of failure.

If you are just learning a technique, you will want to use it only in mildly stressful situations—where you have little at risk and a high likelihood of success. By doing so, you increase your odds of doing it effectively and of gaining the confidence and skill you need to use it in more stressful situations.

For example, when you try to change a situation through assertiveness, you could increase your stress if you have been passive for a long time with a spouse or a boss. If you are a rank beginner at assertiveness, you may jump like lightning from passive to ag- gressive and you may put your job on the line.

Assertiveness requires a lot of practice. Even if your stress is situational, you may need to relax and to think tolerantly about certain situations until you have practiced enough assertiveness in less crucial situations to gain the confidence and skill to speak up in highly stressful ones.

Supplementing Your Formal Techniques

You now understand the three sources of stress and know the limitations of the skills you are just learning. You may also want to supplement the formal techniques with activities you already enjoy.

Let's say you find stress coming from your mind and need relief beyond what your current thought-stopping and changing yield. You might decide to lose yourself temporarily in your favorite thought-occupying activities: reading, working crossword puzzles, playing cards—whatever. If you want to change some stressful im- ages and your imagery skills are not quite strong enough, you might turn to photo albums, TV shows, or movies.

How you handle the stress may also depend on whether you are alone, around people familiar with the *pocket guide*, or with people who might not understand your use of the *guide* in a particular situation.

For example, if you have decided to relax and you can use the *pocket guide* inconspicuously, you might take the quick test with your thumb before and after you relax. If you are alone and have more time, you might use the *pocket guide* for biofeedback.

Order Effects

When you detect unhealthy stress in more than one source, consider using techniques in the following order unless your scan- ning or firing order would dictate otherwise.

If you have identified stress in your body, start there. When you are relaxed, it is easier to change your thoughts and actions. If you have identified mind and situation as your sources of stress, start by changing your thoughts or images. Your actions are then more likely to be calm and considered.

Of course, if the stress is a physical danger, such as a car coming toward you, don't wait to relax and think more clearly before jumping out of the way!

Your Television Debut

If you were asked to make an appearance on TV, would you find it stressful? What sources of stress would your scanning uncover? What techniques would you use to optimize your performance and to relieve your stress?

One of the authors needed instant stress relief when he was invited to appear on TV to promote an earlier book. He certainly considered immediate use of situational techniques numbers two and three on the *pocket guide*: "Escape from the problem," and "Plan how to avoid, reduce, or correct the problem in the future." However, the author scanned body, mind, and situation to identify the sources of stress and decided to take on the challenge by relieving stress before and during the show.

Scanning his body, the author found tension and planned to use a six-second tranquilizer each time the host asked a question. He knew he would understand the questions better and communicate more effectively when relaxed.

Scanning his mind, the author found many self-defeating thoughts and images: "I'm going to make a fool out of myself," and "If I make a mistake, millions of people will be misinformed." He had a week to prepare, so he began using image rehearsals to see himself handling questions in a relaxed and confident way. The author also replaced his initial thoughts with "I'm well prepared and I know what I'm doing" and "Many people will probably benefit from the show."

Focusing on the situation, he assessed his goals. Rather than aim for perfection, he chose to work toward effective communication. Rather than evaluate his performance during the show, he chose to focus all his attention on helping the audience learn about stress. He planned to repeat, "I'm doing very well," whenever evaluative thoughts came to mind.

The author also reduced situational stress by going to the TV station early and using the extra time for a preshow relaxation technique.

After the show, members of the television crew asked the author if he had copies of the book to sell them. One of the hosts wanted to learn more about relaxation training. Each told him how stressful it was to work in television. They really didn't have to convince the author—he was happy just to have survived his first appearance!

Techniques Relieve Stress from More Than One Source

As you can see, solutions for different sources of stress can be combined in exciting and powerful ways. The solutions also overlap, and some relieve stress from more than one source.

Take social support, for example. When we share our innermost thoughts and a friend accepts us with all our faults, the acceptance tends to affirm our healthy self-talk and dispute our negative self-talk.

When you relax, it is a signal to yourself and others that you are calm, in control, and enjoying what you are doing. Relaxation itself often relieves the stress in the situation because relaxation is contagious and attractive to others. It also inspires confident self-talk.

When You're Scanning No Stress

Even if you don't detect any stress from your mind, body, or situation, you may want to practice a technique for stress relief, so you will be prepared to use it when you need it. You may also want to use a technique you have mastered to increase your well-being and your productivity.

The Quieting Response

We would like to share with you one of our favorite combination techniques for refreshing both mind and body. Here is the Quieting Response, by Charles F. Stroebel, M.D., Ph.D.:

The Quieting Response*

1. Smile inwardly and then outwardly with your eyes and mouth.
2. Say to yourself mentally the following self-suggestion: "Alert, amused mind; calm body."
3. Take an easy deep breath.
4. While exhaling breath, let your jaw, tongue, and shoulders go limp; feel a wave of heaviness come over your limbs and muscles; and feel warmth flowing through your body from head to toe (especially imagine warmth flowing into your hands).
5. Resume relaxed, productive living.

Overcoming Obstacles to Lifelong Change

We have encouraged you to select stress relief strategies which are fun and rewarding for you. This approach should help you to use and benefit from these strategies for the rest of your life.

To prevent a return to stressful habits, we also recommend identifying and preparing for those difficult situations and frustrating periods that may threaten continued use. Instant preplay is a very good way to prepare. Use it to imagine overcoming obstacles with change-maintaining thoughts and behaviors.

If you have a relapse, use positive self-talk to remind yourself that "few people ever fail, they just stop trying." Then get back on your feet, review your reasons for making the change, and reward yourself for your efforts.

To help you better understand how to put the power of instant stress relief into daily and lifelong practice, we would like to introduce you to three people and let you look over their shoulders as they use the system to enhance their lives.

36

How Three People Use the Stress-Relief System

You may want to take out your *pocket guide* and refer to it as we describe some of the ways three people use instant stress relief to optimize their health, productivity, and pleasure.

A Young Executive Calmly Climbs the Corporate Ladder

Jack is a junior executive in charge of advertising and marketing for a large firm. We find him seated alone in the waiting room of a major food corporation.

In about ten minutes, he will make a formal presentation to a board meeting in the hopes of attracting the company as a new account. He is not particularly conscious of being nervous about the upcoming meeting, but when he looks at his watch he remembers that he has been using it as a reminder to scan.

Jack prefers to scan in the following order: situation, body, and mind. First, he looks at the room around him and checks his five senses. The room is pleasantly decorated, the temperature is comfortable, and there is soft music in the background.

Next, he moves on to scan his body. He starts at the top of his head but finds no tension in his scalp, face, jaw, and neck. He notices that his shoulders are a little tense and his breathing a little shallow. He has been tapping his fingertips on the arm of the chair, but he is not sweating, his heartbeat is regular, and he has no tension from his waist down.

Jack removes his *pocket guide* from his wallet and puts his thumb on the sensors. He silently and slowly counts to ten.

When he removes his finger, the number 3 sensor square is blue in color. He reads below the sensor that he is "stressed" and looks up 3 above the color blue to find 84 degrees F. The tension in his shoulders and his quick test indicate that he is not relaxed.

Next, Jack scans his mind. He finds that he is a little worried and impatient.

Having detected tension in his body and mind, Jack opens his *pocket guide* to the center section and starts with the first three steps of the body prescriptions to relax and to breathe more deeply. The number 2 sensor square turns yellow, and he is "partly relaxed" at 86 degrees F.

Jack catches himself looking at his watch again and mentally yells, "Stop!" He tells himself, "I'm well prepared and I know what I'm doing." When he checks the mind prescriptions of the *pocket guide*, he is pleased that he remembered the techniques he just used for his mental stress.

On the *pocket guide*, he also sees a key word that he wrote there to remind him of his fondest memory—*ceremony*. Immediately, his mind goes back to the company awards ceremony and his promotion to vice-president.

Jack remembers hearing the president of the company describe his accomplishments. Instantly, he recaptures his feelings of pride, enthusiasm, and confidence.

Feeling more relaxed and confident, Jack decides to use some image rehearsal rather than to waste the time before the meeting. He preplays the meeting and how he will improve his performance with brief relaxation, positive thinking, and assertiveness.

Then he considers taking a mini-vacation to Bermuda in his mind, but decides he is relaxed enough and looks at a news magazine until the secretary calls him in for the meeting.

Yes, Jack made an outstanding presentation and got the account.

But regardless of the outcome, he had relieved unnecessary stress and improved his performance.

Gray Power: Grandmother Learns to Say No without Guilt

Sara is a middle-age grandmother with several adorable grandchildren. It is the afternoon of her weekly bridge party and she is looking forward to seeing her friends. The telephone rings.

It is her newly divorced daughter whose babysitter is sick. She has an important meeting to attend and asks if she can bring the children over for babysitting.

Sara has a number of thoughts and feelings. On one hand, she understands the plight of her daughter, but she knows that she can not babysit for three young children and play bridge at the same time. It is too late to call the other players to cancel; they will be arriving any minute. Besides, she doesn't want to cancel—this is one of the highlights of her week.

Sara scans and finds that she is tense, irritated, and frustrated by her daughter's request. In the past, she always felt guilty about disappointing others and seldom said no.

After a long moment of relaxed silence, she says, "Sweetheart, I know your meeting is important to you and ordinarily I would love to keep the kids, but my weekly bridge party is about to begin, so I will not be able to help you out."

When there is no reply, Sara asks, "Have you thought about dropping the children off at the day-care center?" Her daughter replies that she had thought about that, but it was toward the end of the month and she did not have the money.

Using the assertiveness skills she has learned, Sara firmly replies, "Well darling, I'll be happy to loan you the money. Why don't you drop by and pick up the money on your way?" Her daughter agrees and everyone feels better.

After hanging up the phone, Sara scans and feels quite pleased with her handling of a stressful situation. She finds no lingering tension in her body or her mind, just pleasure at having used her new skills to ward off what would have been a very upsetting situation in the past. She silently congratulates herself.

Sara has some time before the other ladies in the bridge club arrive. She decides to do some biofeedback because she hopes to be able to reduce her dosage of blood pressure medicine. She also likes to use the bridge party as a reward for working on her relaxation skills.

She places her right index finger under the sensor cells of the *pocket guide* and notices that cell number 1 is the lowest-numbered cell displaying a color other than black. It is green, and she reads her skin temperature as approximately 92 degrees.

Sara knows that the "very relaxed" interpretation for sensor cell 1 is not completely accurate because she is taking heart medication. However, she also knows that the card is still useful for biofeedback training because relative changes will still reflect relaxation and health enhancement.

Sara sits down, watches the stress sensor cells, and begins forming warm images in her mind.

After about a minute, the first cell turns turquoise, then blue, and, after a few minutes, violet. She looks at the color chart again and notes that she has raised her temperature three degrees. Having completed a successful biofeedback session, Sara gets up and starts putting out the cards.

With her doctor's approval, Sara has practiced the techniques in this book for six months. She is making progress with assertiveness and her daily biofeedback is paying off. One month later, her doctor is pleased to reduce her blood pressure medication to almost a half of what she was taking before she began relieving her stress.

A Calm and Productive Construction Supervisor

Joe is a busy construction supervisor who spends just as much time driving from job site to job site as he does at his desk in his office. Joe has read about coronary-prone Type A behavior. He is aware that his feeling of being rushed and his anger at any delay on a project are harmful to his health. He decides to learn instant stress relief to help him slow down and to control his tendency to go into "overstrive."

At first, Joe is so busy that he finds it difficult to remember to scan. At the end of the day, he looks back and sees how obsessed he has been with time and deadlines.

To help remind himself, he writes the word *scan* on Scotch tape and puts it on his watch, the clock in his office, and, most importantly, on the rear-view mirror of his car.

Two parts of the instant stress-relief system are particularly useful to Joe. The first is changing his hurry-up thoughts and replacing them with "slow down" self-talk. While driving his car, he scans, finds hurry-up feelings, and talks to himself about slowing down.

Joe's self-talk goes like this: "Slow down. Where's the fire? There's no real emergency. If I get there a few minutes earlier or a few minutes later, it really won't matter. If it really matters, then I need to delegate more effectively, not try to be on top of everything all the time. Is getting there on time worth dying for? I'm going to take my three deep breaths and relax my muscles from head to toe."

Joe always knew he has a stressful job, but he begins to see that the distractions and missed deadlines are partly due to poor time management. To remove this situational stress, he attends a seminar about time management and reads a book about it. He spends some time planning, rearranges some of his procedures, and begins to feel more in control of his time.

The work on mental and situational stress reduce a great deal of Joe's Type-A behavior, so that when he scans during an average work day, he usually finds stress only in his body.

Over a period of three months he is able to learn rapid relaxation techniques through biofeedback to manage his body tension better.

At the office, Joe begins using six-second tranquilizers whenever he answers the phone. He also uses biofeedback or takes a short walk just before lunch. He finds these strategies help him eat more slowly, enjoy his food, and suffer less indigestion. The benefits of the stress relief system are many.

Reviewing the increased construction planned for the summer, Joe becomes concerned. He knows the extra work may disrupt his new routine. Joe uses instant preplay to imagine ways of applying his new skills successfully even during his busy season. Joe is on his way to lifelong stress relief.

37

If You Get Stuck, Want to Learn More, or Want to Help Others

I n about 90 days, most people with average stress levels can master the stress-relief system. They use it frequently and almost automatically. By 120 days, they apply the system routinely and without the *pocket guide.*

Making changes takes time, so don't get discouraged. Remember, learning to manage stress is like learning to drive a car with a stick shift and a clutch—awkward at first but becoming smooth and almost automatic with practice. If you scan and use the instant stress-relief techniques regularly, your health and productivity will improve.

Just as there are limits to instant foods, there are limits to instant stress techniques. Just consider the obvious differences between instant rice and high-protein enriched rice.

Seeking Professional Help

Psychotherapy, counseling, and stress-management training can often be far richer and fulfilling than self-help. Choosing between short-term therapy and long-term therapy is a little like choosing between fast food and gourmet dining.

If you have high stress levels and do not make significant progress on your own in three or four months, then you may need professional help. There are many reasons why people do not make healthy changes.

Sometimes, there are some leftover conflicts from childhood. As Dr. Bernard Siegel, a surgeon, says, "If you love yourself, you'll change. If you are not changing, find out why you don't love yourself."

A professional stress consultation may involve an interview as well as computerized or other testing. Recommendations may include either formal stress-management training or psychotherapy, in a group or alone. You can always return to this guide later to reinforce and to maintain the changes you make in treatment.

Computerized stress testing is widely available through professionals and even by mail order. The computerized assessment closest to the approach taken in this book was developed by one of the authors, Dr. Thomas Staats. It is available to individuals, professionals, and industry from Medicomp, Inc., 1805 Line Avenue, Shreveport, Louisiana 71101; or by calling (318) 424-0752.

If you or your physician want the names and addresses of professionals who provide formal stress-management training and biofeedback in your area, you can contact the Biofeedback Society of America, 10200 West 44th Avenue, Suite 304, Wheat Ridge, Colorado 80033; or call (303) 422-8436. The society maintains a current directory of certified professionals who offer biofeedback training and other stress-management services.

Another national source of information about stress management is the American Institute of Stress, 124 Park Avenue, Yonkers, New York 10703; (914) 963-1200. If you or your doctor have technical questions about stress or the legitimacy of a stress-management approach, organization, or program, the institute will give you the latest scientific information and evaluations available.

Recommended Readings, Recordings, and Services

To help you learn more about the techniques in this guide and other useful approaches to stress management, we have prepared appendix II.

Appendix II lists recommended books, tapes, and monthly digests by the source of stress for which they are most useful. It also lists professional services by the source of stress most likely to be relieved.

Understanding and Helping Others Cope with Stress

People under stress or in crisis may be difficult to work with or live with. Rather than taking the things they do or say personally, remember that the pain a person causes others is often in direct proportion to the pain that person is experiencing.

Frequently, we are asked what to do if friends or loved ones are in distress but will not seek the help they need. Nagging almost never works. One of the best things you can do is to commit yourself quietly to improving the way you relieve stress.

As you change, you will offer an example for the person you want to help. Using the *pocket guide* while he or she is around may give you an opportunity to share your new knowledge, but be careful not to overdo it. Your growth alone will shake up old, unhealthy patterns of interactions. Thus, as you change, the person you want to help must adjust and change as well.

You may also want to give those in distress a copy of this book or leave one in a place where they might read it without admitting they have problems. In addition, you might invite them to come with you to a stress-management seminar or workshop.

If friends or family members become interested and ask for your help, avoid reminding them of what they should be doing. Instead, catch them doing something right and let them know how great it is that they are relieving their stress. If words of praise seem to get misinterpreted, give them a hug or a smile and say nothing.

Don't Be a Stranger

We hope we have been of help to you. Please don't be a stranger. Write us at the address on the card. Tell us of your progress and your favorite instant-stress solutions.

If we were magicians, we would give you the instant praise you deserve for every step you take toward greater health and happiness.

APPENDIX I

Percentile Tables for the Seven-Minute Stress Test

TABLE A

Stress in Your *Situation* Scale:
Raw Score to Percentile Score Conversions

RAW SCORE	PERCENTILE SCORE
42	7
43–44	8
45–46	10
47–48	12
49–50	14
51–53	16
54–56	18
57	21
58–59	24
60–61	27
62–63	31
64–65	34

RAW SCORE	PERCENTILE SCORE
66–67	38
68–69	42
70–71	46
72–73	50
74–76	54
77–78	58
79–80	62
81–82	66
83–84	69
85–86	73
87–88	76
89–90	79
91–92	82
93–94	84
95–97	86
98–99	88
100–101	90
102–103	92
104–105	93
106–107	95
108–111	96
112–113	97
114–118	98
119–126	99
127–134	99.5
135+	99.9

NOTE: The Situation Scale score correlates .84 with the External Stressor Index of the Stress Vector Analysis Test Battery. It also predicts 22 percent of the variance in life intrusive pathology. Such pathology results in impaired personal productivity and a lowered quality of life.

TABLE B
Stress in Your *Body* Scale:
Raw Score to Percentile Score Conversions

RAW SCORE	PERCENTILE SCORE
11	16
12–13	18
14	21
15–16	24
17–18	27
19	31
20–21	34
22	38
23–24	42
25–26	46
27	50
28–29	54
30	58
31–32	62
33–34	66
35	69
36–37	73
38	76
39–40	79
41–42	82
43	84
44–45	86
46	88
47–48	90
49–50	92
51	93
52–53	95
54–56	96
57–58	97
59–61	98
62–67	99

RAW SCORE	PERCENTILE SCORE
68–74	99.5
75+	99.9+

NOTE: The Body Scale score correlates .85 with the Somatogenic Stressor Index of the Stress Vector Analysis Test Battery. It also predicts 81 percent of the variance in physical symptoms.

TABLE C
Stress in Your *Mind* Scale:
Raw Score to Percentile Score Conversions

RAW SCORE	PERCENTILE SCORE
10	8
11	10
12	12
13	16
14	18
15	21
16	24
17	27
18	31
19	38
20	42
21	46
22	50
23	54
24	62
25	66
26	69
27	73
28	76
29	82
30	84
31	86

RAW SCORE	PERCENTILE SCORE
32	88
33	90
34	92
35	95
36	96
37	96
38	97
39	98
40–43	99
44–46	99.5
47+	99.9+

NOTE: The Mind Scale score correlates .81 with the Psychological Stressor Index of the Stress Vector Analysis Test Battery. It also predicts 66 percent of the variance in psychological symptoms.

TABLE D
Total Stress Level:
Sum of Percentiles to Average
Percentile Rank Conversions

SUM OF PERCENTILES	AVERAGE PERCENTILE
30–32	10
33–35	11
36–38	12
39–41	13
42–44	14
45–47	15
48–50	16
51–53	17
54–56	18
57–59	19
60–62	20
63–65	21

SUM OF PERCENTILES	AVERAGE PERCENTILE
66–68	22
69–71	23
72–74	24
75–77	25
78–80	26
81–83	27
84–86	28
87–89	29
90–92	30
93–95	31
96–98	32
99–101	33
102–104	34
105–107	35
108–110	36
111–113	37
114–116	38
117–119	39
120–122	40
123–125	41
126–128	42
129–131	43
132–134	44
135–137	45
138–140	46
141–143	47
144–146	48
147–149	49
150–152	50
153–155	51
156–158	52
159–161	53
162–164	54
165–167	55

SUM OF PERCENTILES	AVERAGE PERCENTILE
168–170	56
171–173	57
174–176	58
177–179	59
180–182	60
183–185	61
186–188	62
189–191	63
192–194	64
195–197	65
198–200	66
201–203	67
204–206	68
207–209	69
210–212	70
213–215	71
216–218	72
219–221	73
222–224	74
225–227	75
228–230	76
231–233	77
234–236	78
237–239	79
240–242	80
243–245	81
246–248	82
249–251	83
252–254	84
255–257	85
258–260	86
261–263	87
264–266	88
267–269	89

SUM OF PERCENTILES	AVERAGE PERCENTILE
270–272	90
273–275	91
276–278	92
279–281	93
282–284	94
285–287	95
288–290	96
291–293	97
294–296	98
297–299	99
300	100

NOTE: The Total Stress score correlates .93 with the overall Stress Vector Score of the Stress Vector Analysis Test Battery. It also predicts 59 percent of the variance in combined life-intrusive pathology, physical symptoms, and mental symptoms.

APPENDIX II

Recommended Books and Recordings

Stress from Your Body

BOOKS

Benson, H., with Klipper, M. *The Relaxation Response.* New York: Avon, 1975.

Charlesworth, E. A., and Nathan, R. G. *Stress Management: A Comprehensive Guide to Wellness.* New York: Ballantine, 1985.

Davis, M., McKay, M. and Eshelman, E. R. *The Relaxation and Stress Reduction Workbook.* California: New Harbinger Publications, 1980.

RECORDINGS

Charlesworth, E. A. Tape 1: "Progressive and Deep Muscle Relaxation;" Tape 2: "Autogenic Relaxation: Arms and Hands, Legs and Feet." From *The Relaxation and Stress Management Program.* Houston: Stress Management Research Associates, 1981.

Stroebel, C. *Quieting Reflex Training For Adults.* New York: BMA Audio Cassettes, 1983.

Stress from Your Mind

BOOKS

Eliot, R. S., and Breo, D. L. *Is It Worth Dying For?* New York: Bantam, 1984.

Ellis, A., and Harper, R. *A New Guide to Rational Living.* Los Angeles: Wilshire, 1975.

RECORDINGS

Charlesworth, E. A. Tape 3: "Visual Imagery Relaxation and Image Rehearsal Practice." From *The Relaxation and Stress Management Program.* Houston: Stress Management Research Associates, 1981.

Dyer, W. *How to be a No-Limit Person.* Chicago: Nightingale-Conant, 1980.

Schuller, R. H. *Possibility Thinking.* Chicago: Nightingale-Conant, 1981.

Waitley, D. E. *The Psychology of Winning.* Chicago: Nightingale-Conant, 1981.

Stress from Your Situation

BOOKS

Alberti, R. E., and Emmons, M. L. *Stand Up, Speak Out, Talk Back!* New York: Pocket Books, 1975.

Blanchard, K., and Johnson, S. *The One Minute Manager.* New York: Berkley, 1983.

Bliss, E. C. *Getting Things Done.* New York: Dell, 1978.

Bloom, L., Coburn, K., and Pearlman, J. *The New Assertive Woman.* New York: Dell, 1976.

RECORDINGS

Alberti, R. E. *Making Yourself Heard: A Guide to Assertive Relationships.* New York: BMA Audio Cassettes, 1986.

Rakos, R. E., and Shroeder, H. *Self-Directed Assertiveness Training.* New York: BMA Audio Cassettes, 1980.

Sources of Ideas in All Three Areas of Stress Relief

MAGAZINE (monthly)

Reader's Digest. Pleasantville, New York: The Reader's Digest Association, Inc.

RECORDING (monthly)

Insight with Earl Nightingale and guests. Chicago: Nightingale-Conant.

Mail Order Resources

BMA Audio Cassettes, a division of Guilford Publications, 200 Park Avenue South, New York, NY 10003; (800) 221-3966, (212) 674-1900.

Nightingale-Conant Corporation, 7300 North Lehigh Avenue, Chicago, IL 60648; (800) 323-5552, (312) 674-0300.

Stress Management Research Associates, Inc., 9725 Louedd Avenue, Houston, TX 77070; (713) 890-8575.

Stress-Relief Techniques Available from Health Care Providers

STRESS FROM YOUR BODY

Medication
Biofeedback Training
Behavior Therapy
Dietary Counseling
Exercise Counseling
Pressure Point Massage

STRESS FROM YOUR SITUATION

Marital/Family Therapy
Assertiveness Training
Career Counseling
Organizational Development
Leisure Counseling

STRESS FROM YOUR MIND

Psychotherapy/Counseling
Medication
Hypnosis
Cognitive Behavior Therapy
Pastoral Counseling

Figure 14: Biofeedback chart

BIOFEEDBACK PRACTICE CHART

APPROACH USED TO RELAX:	MINUTES PRACTICED:	TEMPERATURE BEFORE:	AFTER:
EXAMPLE:			
0. *Image: Relaxing in warm tub.*	4	84 °F	86 °F
1.		°F	°F
2.		°F	°F
3.		°F	°F
4.		°F	°F
5.		°F	°F
6.		°F	°F
7.		°F	°F

Additional Pocket Guides

If you damage your pocket guide, lose it or want to get one for a friend, additional cards are available for $3.95 each. Send a check or money order made out to DPC, Inc., along with a self-addressed, stamped envelope to 3300 Virginia Avenue #2, Shreveport, LA 71103. Please allow up to four weeks for delivery. Quantity discounts are also available.